The ART
of FICTION

The ART of FICTION

Notes on Craft for Young Writers

John Gardner

ALFRED A. KNOPF   NEW YORK   1984

Grateful acknowledgment is made to the following
for permission to reprint previously published material:

Farrar, Straus and Giroux, Inc.: Excerpt from "Views of My Father
Weeping" from City Life, copyright © 1969, 1970 by Donald Barthelme. Reprinted by permission of Farrar, Straus and Giroux, Inc.
This piece first appeared in The New Yorker. Excerpt from "The
Fancy Woman" from The Collected Stories of Peter Taylor, copyright 1941, 1969, renewed 1968 by Peter Taylor. Reprinted by permission of Farrar, Straus and Giroux, Inc.

Random House, Inc.: Excerpt from Seven Gothic Tales, by Isak
Dinesen, copyright 1934 by Harrison Smith and Robert Haas, Inc.,
copyright renewed 1962 by Isak Dinesen. Reprinted by permission of
Random House, Inc. From the Introduction to Superfiction or the
American Story Transformed: An Anthology, by Joe David Bellamy,
copyright © 1975 by Joe David Bellamy. Reprinted by permission of
Random House, Inc.

Simon & Schuster: Excerpt from The Gentleman from San Francisco
by Ivan Bunin, translated by Olga Shartse, copyright © 1963 by
Washington Square Press, Inc. Reprinted by permission of Simon &
Schuster.

Library of Congress Cataloging in Publication Data
Gardner, John, 1933–
The art of fiction.
1. Fiction—Technique. I. Title.
PN3355.G34 1984 808.3 83-47850
ISBN 0-394-50469-0

Manufactured in the United States of America
Published January 19, 1984
Reprinted Five Times

*To all my creative-writing students, and
to all my fellow teachers of creative writing*

Contents

Preface

This is a book designed to teach the serious beginning writer the art of fiction. I assume from the outset that the would-be writer using this book can become a successful writer if he wants to, since most of the people I've known who wanted to become writers, knowing what it meant, *did* become writers. About all that is required is that the would-be writer understand clearly what it is that he wants to become and what he must do to become it. If no matter how hard he tries he simply cannot do what he must do, this book will help him understand why he was not sent into the world to be a writer but for some other noble purpose. Books on writing tend to make much of how difficult it is to become a successful writer, but the truth is that, though the ability to write well is partly a gift—like the ability to play basketball well, or to outguess the stock market—writing ability is mainly a product of good teaching supported by a deep-down love of writing. Though learning to write takes time and a great deal of practice, writing up to the world's ordinary standards is fairly easy. As a matter of fact, most of the books one finds in drugstores, supermarkets, and even small-town public libraries are not well written at all; a smart chimp with a good creative-writing teacher and a real love of sitting around banging a typewriter could have written books vastly more interesting and elegant. Most grown-up behavior, when you come right down to it, is decidedly second-class. People don't drive their cars as well, or wash their ears as well, or eat as well, or even play the harmonica as well as they would if they had sense. This is not to say people are terrible and should be replaced by machines; people are excellent and admirable creatures; efficiency isn't everything. But for the serious young writer who wants to get published, it is encouraging to know that most of the professional writers out there are push-overs.

The instruction here is not for every kind of writer—not for the writer of nurse books or thrillers or porno or the cheaper sort of sci-fi—though it is true that what holds for the most serious kind of fiction will generally hold for junk fiction as well. (Not everyone is capable of writing junk fiction: It requires an authentic junk mind. Most creative-writing teachers have had the experience of occasionally helping to produce, by accident, a pornographer. The most elegant techniques in the world, filtered through a junk mind, become elegant junk techniques.) What is said here, whatever use it may be to others, is said for the elite; that is, for serious literary artists.

The instruction is presented in two somewhat overlapping parts. In Part One, I present a general theory of fiction, a much closer look at what fiction is—what it does, how it works—than is usual in books on craft. Understanding very clearly what fiction "goes for," how it works as a mode of thought, in short what the art of fiction *is*, is the first step toward writing well. In Part Two, I deal with specific technical matters and offer writing exercises.

Needless to say, neither section of this book is exhaustive. I have included here everything that, over the years, I have found it necessary to say as a creative-writing teacher. Some things ultimately of great importance I have found it not necessary to say; so they are not in this book. Let me give an example. The skillful writer may play games with narrative styles and points of view. He may, for instance, use the tone of the old German tale-teller ("At the turn of the century, in the province of D———, there lived . . ."), and he may use that tone, which suggests great authority, in a story where in the end we discover the narrator to be unreliable. For the writer who has thoroughly digested the principles offered in this book, it should be unnecessary to call attention to what the weirdly ironic use of tone and style must do to the narrative. Seize the trunk of any science securely, and you have control of its branches.

I may as well add that I do not give much emphasis here to the various forms of unconventional fiction now popular in universities. Since metafiction is by nature a fiction-like critique of conventional fiction, and since so-called deconstructive fiction (think of Robert Coover's story "Noah's Brother") uses conventional methods, it seems to me more important that young writers understand conventional fiction in all its complexity than that they be too much distracted from the fundamental.

This book and the exercises at the end of it have been used for many years in the various universities where I've taught creative writing, most recently SUNY-Binghamton, and at the Bread Loaf Writers' Conference, and at universities where friends of mine have taught creative writing. In its underground designation as "The Black Book," it has had a wide circulation among writers and teachers, most of them not people I know, friends of friends. I've gotten periodic comments on the book's effectiveness, and at the advice of others who have used it I've revised both the main text and the exercises again and again. I do not publish it now because it seems to me to have at last reached perfection—for all I know, all the changes may have made it a hymn to confusion—but because I'm convinced that in its present stage it's good enough and, so far as I'm aware, the most helpful book of its kind.

In some earlier versions, I had an opening section on how creative writing ought to be taught—the proper use of in- and out-of-class exercises, how much should be required of students, what the proper tone of a workshop should be, and so forth. I thought the discussion important because of the widespread mistaken notion that "creative writing cannot really be taught," an opinion often expressed even by creative-writing teachers. In the end I've dropped that section since it lies outside the domain of this book, which is simply how to write fiction. Anyone interested in hearing my opinions on matters more tangential, from how one should conduct a writers' workshop to whether one should write with a pencil, a pen, or a typewriter, can find them in another book of mine (answers to questions most commonly asked after readings or lectures), *On Becoming a Novelist*.

I

NOTES ON
LITERARY-AESTHETIC
THEORY

I

Aesthetic Law
and Artistic Mystery

What the beginning writer ordinarily wants is a set of rules on
what to do and what not to do in writing fiction. As we'll see,
some general principles can be set down (Things to Think
About When Writing Fiction) and some very general warnings
can be offered (Things to Watch Out For); but on the whole
the search for aesthetic absolutes is a misapplication of the
writer's energy. When one begins to be persuaded that certain
things must never be done in fiction and certain other things
must always be done, one has entered the first stage of aesthetic arthritis, the disease that ends up in pedantic rigidity
and the atrophy of intuition. Every true work of art—and thus
every attempt at art (since things meant to be similar must
submit to one standard)—must be judged primarily, though
not exclusively, by its own laws. If it has no laws, or if its laws
are incoherent, it fails—usually—on that basis.

Trustworthy aesthetic universals do exist, but they exist at
such a high level of abstraction as to offer almost no guidance
to the writer. Most supposed aesthetic absolutes prove relative
under pressure. They're laws, but they slip. Think, for instance,
of the well-known dictum that all expectations raised by the
work of fiction must be satisfied, explicitly or implicitly, within

the fiction—the idea, to put it another way, that all legitimate questions raised in the reader's mind must be answered, however subtly, inside the work. Thus, for example, if we are told that a sheriff in a given story has a Ph.D. in philosophy, an expectation is raised that philosophy will somehow help him do his job. If philosophy is never again mentioned in the story, and if the most careful scrutiny of the story reveals no important way in which philosophy has bearing, we feel dissatisfied, annoyed. The story has, we say, loose ends. The writer has done his work carelessly, cynically. We may suspect the worst of him, that he's in it for the money, that he scorns his reader's intelligence, that his shoddy craftsmanship is intentional and malicious—in fact that he ought to be deported. If he pretends to high seriousness—if he writes not a mystery story but something evidently meant to pass as art—we denounce him as a fake, a pretentious, self-deluded donzel. We're not talking here about superficial slips like—in *Absalom, Absalom!*—Faulkner's description of a house as built of, in one passage, wood and, in another place, stone. For mistakes of this kind, as for slips of the tongue, the sympathetic reader makes silent correction. The mistakes that offend in a would-be work of art are serious slips in reasoning, as when some idea or event is introduced that ought to change the outcome but then is forgotten, or never recognized for what it is, by the writer. And so it has come to be axiomatic that a work should answer every question it raises, that all of a work's elements should fulfill themselves. But is it true?

No one will deny that the principle is useful, especially when applied in obvious ways, as in the examples above or when Chekhov shows us the gun ostentatiously loaded in Act One of *The Seagull*. No one will deny that each time a writer believes he's completed a new work, he ought to look it over in the light of this general principle. But the fact remains that the supposed aesthetic law is far from absolute, since from the beginning of time great writers have shown impatience with it.

Every reader of Homer's *Iliad* is stirred to ask whether Achilles really loves Briseus or simply thinks of her—as Agamemnon does—as a war prize. The point is important because it profoundly affects our judgment of Achilles' character. If he both loves Briseus and considers her his rightful prize (as of course she is), we have adequate motivation for his withdrawal from the war, a withdrawal that must result in the death of friends. If he does not love her, he is likely to seem to us petty and vindictive, a sulky child too sensitive, even for a Greek, about his honor. Critical good will and Homer's high valuation of his hero lead us to assume that Achilles does love Briseus—though also, as the twenty-fourth book makes clear, he exaggerates the value of honor of the sort bestowed by others. But except once, briefly, through the mouth and point of view of a secondary character (Achilles' friend Patroklos), Homer refuses any answer to our question. It's as if the whole matter seemed to him beneath epic dignity, mere tea-table gossip. Perhaps, as some scholars have argued, Greek heroes thought it unmanly to care very much about women. Or, on the other hand, perhaps with his deep sense of what is right and his Greek certainty of love's place in the all-embracing order of Zeus (a subject treated in the *Odyssey*), Homer would be shocked by our doubt of his hero's great-heartedness; that is, perhaps he thought Achilles' love went without saying. But whatever his reason, Homer gives us only what Patroklos thinks—or claims he thinks, in a situation that might incline him to lie—and offers, in his own voice, no clue.

Take another, more modern example. In Shakespeare's *Hamlet* we naturally ask how it is that, when shipped off to what is meant to be his death, the usually indecisive prince manages to hoist his enemies with their own petard—an event that takes place off stage and, at least in the surviving text, gets no real explanation. If pressed, Shakespeare might say that he expects us to recognize that the fox out-foxed is an old motif in literature—he could make up the tiresome details if he had to—and that the point throughout is not Hamlet's indecisiveness in general (any prince worth his salt can knock off a pair of his enemy's fawning underlings) but his self-destructive anxiety as he faces a specific metaphysical dilemma, that of violating law for a higher law in an uncertain universe; that is, murdering a step-father and king on the say-so of a ghost. (I simplify, of course. The proofs are clear enough for the rationalist Horatio; but Horatio is not Hamlet. The center of every Shakespearean play, as of all great literature, is character; and it is Hamlet's panic, rage, and indecisiveness that raise the question of what made him act so decisively this once—the question Shakespeare does not answer.) But the explanation I've put in Shakespeare's mouth is probably not the true one. The truth is very likely that almost without bothering to think it out, Shakespeare saw by a flash of intuition that the whole question was unimportant, off the point; and so like Mozart, the white shark of music, he snapped straight to the heart of the matter, refusing to let himself be slowed for an instant by trivial questions of plot logic or psychological consistency— questions unlikely to come up in the rush of drama, though they do occur to us as we pore over the book. Shakespeare's instinct told him, "Get back to the business between Hamlet and Claudius," and, sudden as lightning, he was back.

This refusal to be led off to the trivial is common in great literature, as is its comic opposite, the endlessly elaborated explanation of the obvious we find in, for instance, the opening chapter of *Tristram Shandy*. This is no proof that the general principle with which we began—the principle that a work should in some way give answers to the questions it raises—is valueless. But the example of Homer, Shakespeare, and others does suggest that aesthetic laws can sometimes be suspended. Suspending recognizable aesthetic laws of course means taking risks, and the teacher who wishes to play it safe may say to his students, "That's all right for Shakespeare, but not for a beginner." The trouble with this solution is that it tries to teach the art of fiction by shrinking the art, making it something more manageable but no longer art.

Art depends heavily on feeling, intuition, taste. It is feeling, not some rule, that tells the abstract painter to put his yellow here and there, not there, and may later tell him that it should have been brown or purple or pea-green. It's feeling that makes the composer break surprisingly from his key, feeling that gives the writer the rhythms of his sentences, the pattern of rise and fall in his episodes, the proportions of alternating elements, so that dialogue goes on only so long before a shift to description or narrative summary or some physical action. The great writer has an instinct for these things. He has, like a great comedian, an infallible sense of timing. And his instinct touches every thread of his fabric, even the murkiest fringes of symbolic structure. He knows when and where to think up and spring surprises, those startling leaps of the imagination that characterize all of the very greatest writing.

Obviously this is not to imply that cool intellect is useless to the writer. What Fancy sends, the writer must order by Judgment. He must think out completely, as coolly as any critic, what his fiction means, or is trying to mean. He must complete his equations, think out the subtlest implications of what he's said, get at the truth not just of his characters and action but also of his fiction's form, remembering that neatness can be carried too far, so that the work begins to seem fussy and overwrought, anal compulsive, unspontaneous, and remembering that, on the other hand, mess is no adequate alternative. He must think as cleanly as a mathematician, but he must also know by intuition when to sacrifice precision for some higher good, how to simplify, take short cuts, keep the foreground up there in front and the background back.

The first and last important rule for the creative writer, then, is that though there may be rules (formulas) for ordinary, easily publishable fiction—imitation fiction—there are no rules for real fiction, any more than there are rules for serious

visual art or musical composition. There are techniques—
hundreds of them—that, like carpenter's tricks, can be studied
and taught; there are moral and aesthetic considerations every
serious writer must sooner or later brood on a little, whether or
not he broods in a highly systematic way; there are common
mistakes—infelicities, clodpole ways of doing things—that
show up repeatedly in unsuccessful fiction and can be shown
for what they are by analysis of how they undermine the fiction's intended effects; there are, in short, a great many things
every serious writer needs to think about; but there are no
rules. Name one, and instantly some literary artist will offer us
some new work that breaks the rule yet persuades us. Invention, after all, is art's main business, and one of the great joys of
every artist comes with making the outrageous acceptable, as
when the painter makes sharply clashing colors harmonious or
a writer in the super-realistic tradition introduces—convincingly—a ghost.

This is not to say that no one really knows what fiction is or
what its limits are; it is simply to recognize that the value or
"staying power" of any piece of literature has to do, finally,
with the character and personality of the artist who created
it—his instincts, his knowledge of art and the world, his mastery. Mastery holds fast. What the beginning writer needs,
discouraging as it may be to hear, is not a set of rules but
mastery—among other things, mastery of the art of breaking so-
called rules. When an artist of true authority speaks—someone
like Homer, Dante, Shakespeare, Racine, Dostoevsky, or Melville—we listen, all attention, even if what he says seems at
first a little queer. (At any rate we listen if we're old enough,
experienced enough, so that we know what kinds of things are
boring, juvenile, simple-minded, and what things are not. To
read well, one also needs a certain kind of mastery.)

On reflection we see that the great writer's authority consists
of two elements. The first we may call, loosely, his sane human-
ness; that is, his trustworthiness as a judge of things, a stability

rooted in the sum of those complex qualities of his character and personality (wisdom, generosity, compassion, strength of will) to which we respond, as we respond to what is best in our friends, with instant recognition and admiration, saying, "Yes, you're right, that's how it is!" The second element, or perhaps I should say *force*, is the writer's absolute trust (not blind faith) in his own aesthetic judgments and instincts, a trust grounded partly in his intelligence and sensitivity—his ability to perceive and understand the world around him—and partly in his experience as a craftsman; that is (by his own harsh standards), his knowledge, drawn from long practice, of what will work and what will not.

What this means, in practical terms for the student writer, is that in order to achieve mastery he must read widely and deeply and must write not just carefully but continually, thoughtfully assessing and reassessing what he writes, because practice, for the writer as for the concert pianist, is the heart of the matter. Though the literary dabbler may write a fine story now and then, the true writer is one for whom technique has become, as it is for the pianist, second nature. Ordinarily this means university education, with courses in the writing of fiction, and poetry as well. Some important writers have said the opposite—for instance, Ernest Hemingway, who is quoted as having said that the way for a writer to learn his craft is to go away and write. Hemingway, it may help to remember, went away for free "tutorials" to two of the finest teachers then living, Sherwood Anderson and Gertrude Stein.

It is true that some writers have kept themselves more or less innocent of education, that some, like Jack London, were more or less self-made men; that is, people who scratched out an education by reading books between work-shifts on boats, in logging camps or gold camps, on farms or in factories. It is true that university education is in many ways inimical to the work of the artist: Rarely do painters have much good to say of aestheticians or history-of-art professors, and it's equally un-

common for even the most serious, "academic" writers to look
with fond admiration at "the profession of English." And it's
true, moreover, that life in the university has almost never produced subject matter for really good fiction. The life has too
much trivia, too much mediocrity, too much soap opera, but
consider:

No ignoramus—no writer who has kept himself innocent of
education—has ever produced great art. One trouble with having read nothing worth reading is that one never fully understands the other side of one's argument, never understands that
the argument is an old one (all great arguments are), never
understands the dignity and worth of the people one has cast
as enemies. Witness John Steinbeck's failure in *The Grapes of
Wrath*. It should have been one of America's great books. But
while Steinbeck knew all there was to know about Okies and
the countless sorrows of their move to California to find work,
he knew nothing about the California ranchers who employed
and exploited them; he had no clue to, or interest in, their
reasons for behaving as they did; and the result is that Steinbeck wrote not a great and firm novel but a disappointing
melodrama in which complex good is pitted against unmiti-
gated, unbelievable evil. Objectivity, fair-mindedness, the
systematic pursuit of legitimate evaluation, these are some of
the most highly touted values of university life, and even if—as
is no doubt true—some professors are as guilty of simplification
as John Steinbeck was, the very fact that these values are
mouthed must have some effect on the alert student. Moreover,
no student can get far in any university without encountering
the discussion method; and what this means, at least in any
good university, is that the student must learn to listen carefully and fair-mindedly to opinions different from his own. In
my experience, this is not common elsewhere. In most assem-
blies, people all argue on the same side. Look at small-town
papers. Truth is not much valued where everyone agrees on
what the truth is and no one is handy to speak up for the side

that's been dismissed. However bad university professors may be in general, every great professor is a man or woman devoted to truth, and every university has at least one or two of them around.

But what makes ignoramuses bad writers is not just their inexperience in fair argument. All great writing is in a sense imitation of great writing. Writing a novel, however innovative that novel may be, the writer struggles to achieve one specific large effect, what can only be called the effect we are used to getting from good novels. However weird the technique, whatever the novel's mode, we say when we have finished it, "Now *that* is a *novel!*" We say it of *Anna Karenina* and of *Under the Volcano*, also of the mysteriously constructed *Moby-Dick*. If we say it of Samuel Beckett's *Watt* or *Malone Dies*, of Italo Calvino's *The Baron in the Trees*, or Kobo Abe's *The Ruined Map*, we say it because, for all their surface oddity, those novels produce the familiar effect. It rarely happens, if it happens at all, that a writer can achieve effects much larger than the effects achieved in books he has read and admired. Human beings, like chimpanzees, can do very little without models. One may learn to love Shakespeare by reading him on one's own—the ignoramus is unlikely to have done even this—but there is no substitute for being taken by the hand and guided line by line through *Othello*, *Hamlet*, or *King Lear*. This is the work of the university Shakespeare course, and even if the teacher is a person of limited intelligence and sensitivity, one can find in universities the critical books and articles most likely to be helpful, the books that have held up, and the best of the new books. Outside the university's selective process, one hardly knows which way to turn. One ends up with some crank book on how Shakespeare was really an atheist, or a Communist, or a pen-name used by Francis Bacon. Outside the university it seems practically impossible to come to an understanding of Homer or Vergil, Chaucer or Dante, any of the great masters who, properly understood, provide the highest models yet achieved by our civilization. Whatever his genius, the writer unfamiliar with the highest effects possible is virtually doomed to search out lesser effects.

Admittedly the man who has educated himself is in a better position than the man not educated at all. But his work is sure to bear the mark of his limitation. If one studies the work of the self-educated—and we do not mean here the man who starts out with limited but rigorous and classical education, like Herman Melville—what one notices at once is the spottiness and therefore awkwardness of their knowledge. One forgives the fault, but the fact remains that it distracts and makes the work less than it might have been. One finds, for instance, naively excited and lengthy discussions of ideas that are commonplace or have long been discredited, or one finds curious, quirky interpretations of old myths—interpretations that, though interesting in themselves, suffer by comparison with what the myths really say and mean. We read, let us say, a story about Penelope as a grudging, recalcitrant wife. The writing may be superb, but when we think of Homer's portrait of the true, perfect wife, as courageous, cunning, and devoted as her husband, Homer's version so outshines the new one that we turn almost in disgust from the new writer's work. True, one can as easily get spotty knowledge from university graduates, and one can as easily get crackpot opinions from university professors as from independent study. The success of fools in the university world is one of God's great mysteries. But it's beside the point that the man who's been through university study can have knowledge as spotty as the self-made man's. The university can do no more than offer opportunities— opportunities made available nowhere else: a wealth of books, at least a few first-rate courses, professors, and fellow students, also lectures, debates, readings, and gatherings where anyone at all, if he's not too shy, can talk with some of the best novelists, poets, musicians, painters, politicians, and scientists of the age. If foolishness abounds in universities, it is only within that

same university world that the honest understanding of literature is a conscious discipline. No one can hope to write really
well if he has not learned how to analyze fiction—how to recognize a symbol when it jumps at him, how to make out theme
in a literary work, how to account for a writer's selection and
organization of fictional details.

We need not be much distressed by the fact that as a rule
painters have very little good to say of art historians and
aestheticians, or that writers, even our best-educated writers,
often express impatience with English professors. The critic's
work—that is, the English professor's—is the analysis of what
has already been written. It is his business to systematize what
he reads and to present his discoveries in the way most likely to
be beneficial to his students. If he's good at his job, he does this
more or less dispassionately, objectively. He may be moved by
a particular work, and may let his students know it, but though
tears run down his cheeks, his purpose is to make structure and
meaning crystal clear. This can lead—from the artist's point of
view—to two evils. First, the professor, and indeed his whole
profession, may tend to choose not the best works of literature
but those about which it is most possible to make subtle observations. Since the novels of Anthony Trollope contain almost no obscure allusions and no difficult symbolism, they are
hard to teach. One stands in front of class mouthing platitudes,
snatching about for something interesting to say. On the other
hand, one can dazzle one's students almost endlessly, or encourage one's students to dazzle one another, with talk about
allusion and symbol in the work of ingenious but minor writers.
Subtly and insidiously, standards become perverted. "Good" as
an aesthetic judgment comes to mean "tricky," "academic,"
"obscure."

This perversion of standards leads to the second evil: The
literature program wastes the young writer's time. Instead of
allowing him to concentrate on important books, from Homer's
Iliad to John Fowles' *Daniel Martin*, it clutters his reading

hours with trivia, old and new. To the extent that a given program feels obliged to treat English and American literature in their historical development, the offense is likely to be compounded. Though no one will deny that writers like Thomas Otway or, say, George Crabbe have both their innate and their historical interest, they have no more relevance for the serious young writer than has, for instance, James D. Watson's little book on the discovery of DNA. Probably less.

But the student is no helpless robot in the program. Strange to say—since writers so often speak harshly of English professors—young writers are almost always the darlings of the department, especially if they're good and serious young writers; so that it's almost always possible for the writer to work out some special arrangement, getting the courses he needs and avoiding those likely to be useless to him. (Who can hate a student who wants Dante instead of Dryden, Joyce instead of Jonathan Edwards?) And in any event, no law requires that the student leave college with a degree—discounting practical considerations. All that's required is that the student get, somehow, the literary background he needs.

One last remark and we can end this digression on the importance, for the serious young writer, of formal education.

The argument that what the writer really needs is experience in the world, not training in literature—both reading and writing—has been so endlessly repeated that for many it has come to sound like gospel. We cannot take time for a full answer here—how wide experience, from Zanzibar to the Yukon, is more likely to lead to cluttered texture than to deep and moving fiction, how the first-hand knowledge of a dozen trades is likely to be of less value to the writer than twenty good informants, the kind one gets talking to in bars, on Greyhound buses, at parties, or on sagging park benches. The primary subject of fiction is and has always been human emotion, values, and beliefs. The novelist Nicholas Delbanco has remarked that by the age of four one has experienced nearly everything one needs as a writer of fiction: love, pain, loss, boredom, rage, guilt, fear of death. The writer's business is to make up convincing human beings and create for them basic situations and actions by means of which they come to know themselves and reveal themselves to the reader. For that one needs no schooling. But it's by training—by studying great books and by writing—that one learns to *present* one's fictions, giving them their due. Through the study of technique—not canoeing or logging or slinging hash—one learns the best, most efficient ways of making characters come alive, learns to know the difference between emotion and sentimentality, learns to discern, in the planning stages, the difference between the better dramatic action and the worse. It is this kind of knowledge—to return to our earlier subject—that leads to mastery.

However he may get it, mastery—not a full mental catalogue of the rules—must be the writer's goal. He must get the art of fiction, in all its complexity—the whole tradition and all its technical options—down through the wrinkles and tricky wiring of his brain into his blood. Not that he needs to learn literature first and writing later: The two processes are inseparable. Every real writer has had Melville's experience. He works at the problem of Ahab and the whale (the idea of an indifferent or malevolent universe), he happens to read Shakespeare and some philosophy books at the same time, and because of his reading he hits on heretofore unheard-of solutions to problems of novelistic exploration. Mastery is not something that strikes in an instant, like a thunderbolt, but a gathering power that moves steadily through time, like weather.

In other words, art has no universal rules because each true artist melts down and reforges all past aesthetic law. To learn to write well, one must begin with a clear understanding that for the artist, if not for the critic, aesthetic law is the enemy. To the great artist, anything whatever is possible. Invention, the spontaneous generation of new rules, is central to art. And since one does not learn to be a literary artist by studying first how to be something different from a literary artist, it follows that for the young writer, as for the great writer he hopes to become, there can be no firm rules, no limits, no restrictions. Whatever works is good. He must develop an eye for what—by his own carefully informed standards—works.

2

Basic Skills, Genre, and Fiction as Dream

If there are no rules, or none worth his attention, where is the beginning writer to begin?

Often one glance at the writer's work tells the teacher that what this student writer needs first, before stirring an inch in the direction of fiction, is a review of fundamentals. No one can hope to write well if he has not mastered—absolutely mastered—the rudiments: grammar and syntax, punctuation, diction, sentence variety, paragraph structure, and so forth. It is true that punctuation (for instance) is a subtle art; but its subtlety lies in suspending the rules, as in "You, don't, know, a god, damned, thing," or "He'd seen her before, he was sure of it." No writer should ever have to hesitate for an instant over what the rule to be kept or suspended *is*. If he wishes, the teacher may deal with the student's problems as the course goes along (as one deals with spelling), but this is not at all the best way. Learning to write fiction is too serious a business to be mixed in with leftovers from freshman composition. The teacher, if he knows what he's doing, is too valuable to be wasted in this way; and the student, once he learns that he can get rid of most problems quickly and easily, is certain to want to do so. With the proper help and the proper book, any good student can cover the fundamentals, once and for all, in two weeks. The proper book, in my opinion, is W. W. Watt's *An American Rhetoric*, the most accurate and efficient book on composition available, also the most interesting and amusing. Usually the student can do and correct the exercises himself, though occasionally he may need to take a problem to his teacher. If he finds that he needs help frequently, it's a fairly clear sign that he'll never be a writer.

Let us suppose the writer has mastered the rudiments. How should he begin on fiction? What should he write about, and how can he know when he's done it well?

A common and usually unfortunate answer is "Write about what you know." Nothing can be more limiting to the imagination, nothing is quicker to turn on the psyche's censoring devices and distortion systems, than trying to write truthfully and interestingly about one's own home town, one's Episcopalian mother, one's crippled younger sister. For some writers, the advice may work, but when it does, it usually works by a curious accident: The writer writes well about what he knows because he has read primarily fiction of just this kind—realistic fiction of the sort we associate with *The New Yorker*, the *Atlantic Monthly*, or *Harper's*. The writer, in other words, is presenting not so much what he knows about life as what he knows about a particular literary genre. A better answer, though still not an ideal one, might have been "Write the kind of story you know and like best—a ghost story, a science-fiction piece, a realistic story about your childhood, or whatever."

Though the fact is not always obvious at a glance when we look at works of art very close to us in time, the artist's primary unit of thought—his primary conscious or unconscious basis for selecting and organizing the details of his work—is *genre*. This is perhaps most obvious in the case of music. A composer writes an opera, a symphony, a concerto, a tone poem, a suite of country dances, a song cycle, a set of variations, or a stream-of-consciousness piece (a modern psychological adaptation of

the tone poem). Whatever genre he chooses, and to some extent depending on which genre he chooses, he writes within, or
slightly varies, traditional structures—sonata form, fugal structure, ABCBA melodic structure, and so forth; or he may create,
on what he believes to be some firm basis, a new structure.
He may cross genres, introducing country dances into a symphony or, say, constructing a string quartet on the principle of
theme and variations. If he's looking for novelty (seldom for
any more noble reason), he may try to borrow structure from
some other art, using film, theatrical movement, or something
else. When new forms arise, as they do from time to time, they
rise out of one of two processes, genre-crossing or the elevation
of popular culture. Thus Ravel, Gershwin, Stravinsky, and
many others blend classical tradition and American jazz—in
this case simultaneously crossing genres and elevating the
popular. Occasionally in music as in the other arts, elevating
popular culture must be extended to mean recycling trash.
Electronic music began in the observation that the beeps and
boings that come out of radios, computers, and the like might
sound a little like music if structure were imposed—rhythm
and something like melody. Anything, in fact—as the Dadaists,
Spike Jones, and John Cage pointed out—might be turned into
something like music: the scream of a truck-tire, the noise of a
windowshade, the bleating of a sheep.

　　We see much the same in the visual arts. In any culture
certain subjects become classical, repeated by artist after artist
—for instance, in the Christian Middle Ages, the theme of the
dead Christ's descent from the cross, the martyrdom of St.
Stephen, the mother and child. As the surrounding culture
changes, the treatment of classical subjects changes, popular
culture increasingly impinges, new forms arise—literary illustration replacing Biblical illustration, secular figures paro-
dying religious figures, "real life" edging out illustrative
painting, new ventures of thought (psychology, mathematics)
transforming traditional still lifes, rooms, and landscapes to

dream images or spatial puzzles. The process of change in the visual arts, in other words, is identical to that in music. Sometimes it rises out of genre-crossing, as when Protestant Flemish painters present a secular family portrait in the triangular organization of Catholic holy-family painters; sometimes it rises out of an elevation of the popular, or of trash, as on Giotto's campanile, in Matisse's cut-outs, or in the trash collages of Robert Rauschenberg; and sometimes change comes—the usual case—out of both at once.

The same holds true for literature. Novelty comes chiefly from ingenious genre-crossing or elevation of familiar materials. As an example of genre-crossing, think of the best of the three versions of Faulkner's "Spotted Horses" (the one that begins with the words "That Flem"), where techniques of the yarn—mainly diction, comic exaggeration, and cruel humor—are combined with techniques of the realistic-symbolic short story. Genre-crossing of one sort or another is behind most of the great literary art in the English tradition. Chaucer again and again plays one form off against another, as in the Knight's Tale, where, along with other, less-well-known forms, he blends epic and romance. The greatest of all medieval alliterative poems, Sir Gawain and the Green Knight, blends elements of the earthy fabliau (in the temptation scenes) with romance elements. Shakespeare's most powerful techniques are all results of genre-crossing: his combination of prose and verse to expand the emotional range of drama; his combination of Roman high-style convention with conventions drawn from the English folk plays, rowdy medieval mystery plays (or guild plays), and so on; and his crossing of tragic convention and comic convention for the "dark comedies." Milton's fondness for genre-crossing is one of the commonplaces of scholarship. As for the elevation of popular materials or trash—alone or in combination with nobler forms—think of John Hawkes' blend of the psychological-symbolic novel and the American hard-boiled mystery, Italo Calvino's blend (in t-zero and Cosmi-

comics) of sci-fi, fantasy, comic-book language and imagery, movie melodrama, and nearly everything else, or Donald Barthelme's transformation of such cultural trash as the research questionnaire, the horror-show and animated cartoon, the travelogue and psychiatrist's transcript. Like genre-crossing, the elevation of popular or trash materials is an old and familiar form of innovation. It was a favorite method of late Greek poets like Apollonios Rhodios (in the *Argonautica*), Roman comic poets, many of the great medieval poets (think of Chaucer's *Rime of Sir Thopas*), and poets of the Renaissance. The noblest of modern literary forms, equivalent in range and cultural importance to the noblest of musical forms, the symphony, began in the elevation and transformation of trash when Defoe, Richardson, and Fielding began transmuting junk into art. *Robinson Crusoe* and *Moll Flanders* spring, respectively, from the naive shipwreck narrative and the rogue's confession; *Pamela* and *Clarissa* add character and plot to the popular collection of epistolary models for the guidance of young ladies; *Jonathan Wilde* comes from the gallows broadside, or story of the character and horrible crimes of the felon about to be hanged.

None of these writers, ancient or modern, sat down to write "to express himself." They sat down to write this kind of story or that, or to mix this form with that form, producing some new effect. Self-expression, whatever its pleasures, comes about incidentally. It also comes about inevitably. The realistic writer may set out to conjure up the personality of his aunt, creating for her, or copying from life, some story through which her character is revealed, and thus he reveals his strong feelings about his aunt; that is, he expresses himself. The fabulist—the writer of non-realistic yarns, tales, or fables—may seem at first glance to be doing something quite different; but he is not. Dragons, like bankers and candy-store owners, must have firm and predictable characters. A talking tree, a talking refrigerator, a talking clock must speak in a way we learn to recognize, must influence events in ways we can identify as flowing from some definite motivation; and since character can come only from one of two places, books or life, the writer's aunt is as likely to show up in a fable as in a realistic story. Thus the process by which one writes a fable, on one hand, or a realistic story, on the other, is not much different. Let us look more closely at the similarities and differences.

In any piece of fiction, the writer's first job is to convince the reader that the events he recounts really happened, or to persuade the reader that they might have happened (given small changes in the laws of the universe), or else to engage the reader's interest in the patent absurdity of the lie. The realistic writer's way of making events convincing is verisimilitude. The tale writer, telling stories of ghosts, or shape-shifters, or some character who never sleeps, uses a different approach: By the quality of his voice, and by means of various devices that distract the critical intelligence, he gets what Coleridge called—in one of the most clumsy famous sentences in all literature—"the willing suspension of disbelief for the moment, which constitutes poetic faith." The yarn writer—like Mark Twain in "The Celebrated Jumping Frog of Calaveras County" or "Baker's Bluejay Yarn" —uses yet another method: He tells outrageous lies, or has some character tell the poor narrator some outrageous lie, and he simultaneously emphasizes both the brilliance and the falsehood of the lie; that is, he tells the lie as convincingly as he can but also raises objections to the lie, either those objections the reader might raise or, for comic effect, literal-minded country-bumpkin objections that, though bumpkinish, call attention to the yarn's improbabilities.

All three kinds of writing, it should be obvious at a glance, depend heavily on precision of detail. In writing that depends on verisimilitude, the writer in effect argues the reader into acceptance. He places his story in some actual setting—Cleveland, San Francisco, Joplin, Missouri—and he uses characters we would be likely to meet in the setting he has chosen. He gives us

such detail about the streets, stores, weather, politics, and concerns of Cleveland (or whatever the setting is) and such detail
about the looks, gestures, and experience of his characters that
we cannot help believing that the story he tells us must be true.
In fact it may be true, as is Truman Capote's novel *In Cold
Blood* or Norman Mailer's *The Executioner's Song.* The fact that
the story is true of course does not relieve the novelist of the
responsibility of making the characters and events convincing.
Second by second we ask, "Would a mother really say that?"
"Would a child really think that?" and if the novelist has done
his work well we cannot help answering, "Yes." If he has done
his work badly, on the other hand, the reader feels unconvinced
even when the writer presents events he actually witnessed in
life. What has gone wrong, in this case, is that the writer missed
or forgot to mention something important to the development of
the scene. For instance, if a fictional husband and wife are arguing bitterly and the wife suddenly changes her tactics, speaking gently, even lovingly, the reader cannot understand or
believe the change unless some clue is provided as to the reason
for it. The clue may be an event, perhaps a noise in another part
of the house, that reminds her that the children are nearby; or it
may be a thought, perhaps the wife's reflection that this is how
her mother used to argue with her father; or the clue may be a
gesture, as when the wife, after something the husband says,
turns and looks out the window, providing a pause that allows
her to collect herself. When the realist's work convinces us, all
effects, even the most subtle, have explicit or implicit causes.
This kind of documentation, moment by moment authenticating
detail, is the mainstay not only of realistic fiction but of all
fiction.

In other words, while verisimilar fiction may be described
generally as fiction that persuades us of its authenticity through
real-world documentation, using real or thoroughly lifelike loca-
tions and characters—real cities or cities we believe to be real
although their names have been changed, real-life characters

with actual or substituted names, and so forth—the line-by-line bulk of a realist's work goes far beyond the accurate naming of streets and stores or accurate description of people and neighborhoods. He must present, moment by moment, concrete images drawn from a careful observation of how people behave, and he must render the connections between moments, the exact gestures, facial expressions, or turns of speech that, within any given scene, move human beings from emotion to emotion, from one instant in time to the next.

Compare the technique of the writer of tales. Whereas the realist argues the reader into acceptance, the tale writer charms or lulls him into dropping objections; that is, persuades him to suspend disbelief. Isak Dinesen begins one of her tales: "After the death of his master Leonidas, Angelino Santasillia resolved that he would never again sleep. Will the narrator be believed when he tells the reader that Angelino kept this resolve? Nevertheless, it is the case." No realist, of course, could tell this story, since no amount of argument will convince us that a character really might stay awake for weeks, months, years. The tale writer simply walks past our objections, granting that the events he is about to recount are incredible but winning our suspension of disbelief by the confidence and authority of the narrator's voice. Yet after establishing the impossible premise, one that opens the door to further improbabilities—in the case of Isak Dinesen's tale, as it happens, the appearance of Judas, at the end of the narrative, counting his silver in a small, dimly lit room—the tale writer documents his story moment by moment by details of exactly the kind realists use. The opening lines slightly alter natural law, but granting the alteration, what follows is made to seem thoroughly probable and at least poetically true by the writer's close attention to the natural flow of moral cause and effect, a flow minutely documented with details drawn from life. As the story progresses, the sleepless Angelino walks, talks, and thinks more and more slowly. Sometimes whole days pass between the beginnings and ends of his sentences. We "believe" the narrative not just because the tale voice has charmed us but also, and more basically, because the character's gestures, his precisely described expression, and the reaction of others to his oddity all seem to us exactly what they would be in this strange situation. The images are as sharp and accurately rendered as any in Tolstoy's *Childhood* or *Anna Karenina*. The streets he walks, the weather, the city's sounds and smells all authenticate the sleepless man's existence. There is, admittedly, one great difference between the use of authenticating detail by a realist and the use of the same by a tale writer. The realist must authenticate continually, bombarding the reader with proofs; the writer of tales can simplify, persuading us partly by the beauty or interest of his language, using authenticating detail more sparingly, to give vividness to the tale's key moments. Thus, for example, once the writer of a tale has convinced us, partly by charm, partly by detail, that a certain king has a foul temper, he can make such bald statements as: "The king was furious. He sent everyone home, locked all the doors, and had chains wrapped tight around his castle." Nevertheless the difference is one of degree. Neither the realist nor the writer of tales can get by without documentation through specific detail.

It's the same in the yarn. Consider the following, from Mark Twain's "Baker's Bluejay Yarn."

"When I first begun to understand jay language correctly, there was a little incident happened here. Seven years ago, the last man in this region but me moved away. There stands his house—been empty ever since; a log house, with a plank roof—just one big room, and no more; no ceiling—nothing between the rafters and the floor. Well, one Sunday morning I was sitting out here in front of my cabin, with my cat, taking the sun, and looking at the blue hills, and listening to the leaves rustling so lonely in the trees, and thinking of the home away yonder in the states, that I hadn't heard from in thirteen years, when a bluejay lit on that house, with an acorn in his mouth, and says, 'Hello, I reckon I've struck something.' When he spoke, the acorn dropped out of his mouth and rolled down the roof, of course, but he didn't care; his mind was all on the thing he had struck. It was a knot-hole in the roof. He cocked his head to one side, shut one eye and put the other one to the hole, like a 'possum looking down a jug; then he glanced up with his bright eyes, gave a wink or two with his wings—which signifies gratification, you understand—and says, 'It looks like a hole, it's located like a hole—blamed if I don't believe it *is* a hole!' "

Baker, we understand, has been out in the wilderness too long and has gone a little dotty—or else (more likely) he's pulling the leg of the credulous narrator who reports his story as gospel. Either way, no one but the narrator imagines for a moment that what Baker is saying is true. What makes the lie delightful is the pains Baker takes to make it credible. The cabin with the knot-hole in the roof exists: It has a history and physical features—in fact Baker can point to it. Details convince us that Baker really did sit looking at it: It was a Sunday morning; his cat was with him; he was looking at and listening to specific things, thinking specific thoughts. The bluejay really did speak—the acorn is the proof—and further details labor valiantly to persuade us that bluejays think: the cocked head, the one closed eye, the vivid image of the open eye pressed to the knot-hole "like a 'possum looking down a jug."

In all the major genres, vivid detail is the life blood of fiction. Verisimilitude, suspension of disbelief through narrative voice, or the wink that calls attention to the yarn-teller's lie may be the *outer* strategy of a given work; but in all major genres, the inner strategy is the same: The reader is regularly presented with proofs—in the form of closely observed details—that what is said to be happening is really happening. Before we turn to the technical implications of this fact, let us look, briefly, at a few more examples, since the point is one of great importance. Take a short scene from Peter Taylor's "The Fancy Woman." George has brought Josephine, the "fancy woman" or prostitute he loves, home to meet the family. Josephine has been drinking, and George is determined to sober her up.

As he pushed Josephine onto the white, jumpy beast he must have caught a whiff of her breath. She knew that he must have! He was holding the reins close to the bit while she tried to arrange herself in the flat saddle. Then he grasped her ankle and asked her, "Did you take a drink upstairs?" She laughed, leaned forward in her saddle, and whispered:

"Two. Two jiggers."

She wasn't afraid of the horse now, but she was dizzy. "George, let me down," she said faintly. She felt the horse's flesh quiver under her leg and looked over her shoulder when it stomped one rear hoof.

George said, "Confound it, I'll sober you." He handed her the reins, stepped back, and slapped the horse on the flank. "Hold on!" he called, and her horse cantered across the lawn.

Josie was clutching the leather straps tightly, and her face was almost in the horse's mane. "I could kill him for this," she said, slicing out the words with a sharp breath. God damn it! The horse was galloping along a dirt road. She saw nothing but the yellow dirt. The hoofs crumbled over a three-plank wooden bridge, and she heard George's horse on the other side of her. She turned her face that way and saw George through the hair that hung over her eyes. He was smiling. "You dirty bastard," she said.

Who can doubt the scene? Taylor tells us that the horse is "jumpy" and proves it by a closely observed detail: George holds the reins—as one must to control a jumpy horse when one is standing on the ground—"close to the bit." That Josie is sitting on a real horse, and a jumpy one, is proved by further authenticating details: The horse's flesh quivers "under her leg," and when the writer tells us that Josephine "looked over her shoulder when it stomped one rear hoof," we are at once convinced by both the horse's action and the woman's response. Since Josie is dizzy and presumably not a good rider, we are fully persuaded by the detail telling us "her face was almost in the horse's mane," by the panicky way in which she talks to herself, "slicing out the words with a sharp breath," by the fact that, riding down the dirt road, she "saw nothing but the yellow dirt," by the "three-plank wooden bridge" (in her alarm she looks closely), by the fact that she hears George's horse before she sees it, and by the fact that, turning to look at him, she sees George "through the hair that hung over her eyes." Examining the scene carefully, we discover that something like half of it is devoted to details that prove its actuality.

Compare a short passage from a comic tale in Italo Calvino's *Cosmicomics* (translated from the Italian by William Weaver). The narrator, old Qfwfq, is recalling the days, in the Carboniferous period of the planet, when osseous, pulmonate fish, including Qfwfq, moved up from the sea onto land.

> Our family, I must say, including grandparents, was all up on the shore, padding about as if we had never known how to do anything else. If it hadn't been for the obstinacy of our great-uncle N'ba N'ga, we would have long since lost all contact with the aquatic world.
>
> Yes, we had a great-uncle who was a fish, on my paternal grandmother's side, to be precise, of the Coelacanthus family of the Devonian period (the fresh-water branch: who are, for that matter, cousins of the others—but I don't want to go into all these questions of kinship, nobody can ever follow them anyhow). So as I was saying, this great-uncle lived in certain muddy shallows, among

the roots of some protoconifers, in that inlet of the lagoon where all our ancestors had been born. He never stirred from there: at any season of the year all we had to do was push ourselves over the softer layers of vegetation until we could feel ourselves sinking into the dampness, and there below, a few palms' lengths from the edge, we could see the column of little bubbles he sent up, breathing heavily the way old folks do, or the little cloud of mud scraped up by his sharp snout, always rummaging around, more out of habit than out of the need to hunt for anything.

Partly we believe, or forget to disbelieve, what Calvino tells us because of the charm of old Qfwfq's voice; and partly we're convinced by vivid detail. I will not labor the point—the fish-animals "padding about" on shore, the vivid picturing of great-uncle N'ba N'ga's home (the muddy shallows among the roots of protoconifers), the vivid image of the fish-animals pushing themselves "over the softer layers of vegetation until we could feel ourselves sinking into the dampness," the specificity and appropriateness of the measure "a few palms' lengths," the column of little bubbles, the great-uncle's habit of "breathing heavily the way old folks do," the "little cloud of mud scraped up by his sharp snout, always rummaging around, more out of habit than out of the need to hunt for anything."

Consider, finally, the piling up of authenticating details in Ivan Bunin's "The Gentleman from San Francisco," a more conventionally narrated, serious tale. The passage presents an ocean liner crossing the Atlantic.

On the second and third night there was again a ball—this time in mid-ocean, during the furious storm sweeping over the ocean, which roared like a funeral mass and rolled up mountainous seas fringed with mourning silvery foam. The Devil, who from the rocks of Gibraltar, the stony gateway of two worlds, watched the ship vanish into night and storm, could hardly distinguish from behind the snow the innumerable fiery eyes of the ship. The Devil was as huge as a cliff, but the ship was even bigger, a many-storied, many-stacked giant. . . . The blizzard battered the ship's rigging and its broad-necked stacks, whitened with snow, but it remained firm, majestic— and terrible. On its uppermost deck, amidst a snowy whirlwind there loomed up in loneliness the cozy, dimly lighted cabin, where, only half awake, the vessel's ponderous pilot reigned over its entire mass, bearing the semblance of a pagan idol. He heard the wailing moans and the furious screeching of the siren, choked by the storm, but the nearness of that which was behind the wall and which in the last account was incomprehensible to him, removed his fears. He was reassured by the thought of the large, armored cabin, which now and then was filled with mysterious rumbling sounds and with the dry creaking of blue fires, flaring up and exploding around a man with a metallic headpiece, who was eagerly catching the indistinct voices of the vessels that hailed him, hundreds of miles away. . . .

One can see at a glance that the details are symbolic, identifying the ship as a kind of hell constructed by the pride of modern man and more terrible than the power of the Devil. But my point at the moment is only this: that here too, as everywhere in good fiction, it's physical detail that pulls us into the story, makes us believe or forget not to believe or (in the yarn) accept the lie even as we laugh at it.

If we carefully inspect our experience as we read, we discover that the importance of physical detail is that it creates for us a kind of dream, a rich and vivid play in the mind. We read a few words at the beginning of the book or the particular story, and suddenly we find ourselves seeing not words on a page but a train moving through Russia, an old Italian crying, or a farm-house battered by rain. We read on—dream on—not passively but actively, worrying about the choices the characters have to make, listening in panic for some sound behind the fictional door, exulting in characters' successes, bemoaning their failures. In great fiction, the dream engages us heart and soul; we not only respond to imaginary things—sights, sounds, smells—as though they were real, we respond to fictional problems as though they were real: We sympathize, think, and judge. We act out, vicariously, the trials of the characters and learn from the failures and successes of particular modes of action, particu-lar attitudes, opinions, assertions, and beliefs exactly as we learn from life. Thus the value of great fiction, we begin to suspect, is not just that it entertains us or distracts us from our troubles, not just that it broadens our knowledge of people and places, but also that it helps us to know what we believe, reinforces those qualities that are noblest in us, leads us to feel uneasy about our faults and limitations.

This is not the place to pursue that suspicion—that is, the place to work out in detail the argument that the ultimate value of fiction is its morality, though the subject is one we must return to—but it is a good place to note a few technical implica-tions of the fact that, whatever the genre may be, fiction does its work by creating a dream in the reader's mind. We may observe, first, that if the effect of the dream is to be powerful, the dream must probably be vivid and continuous—*vivid* because if we are not quite clear about what it is that we're dreaming, who and where the characters are, what it is that they're doing or trying to do and why, our emotions and judgments must be confused, dissipated, or blocked; and *continuous* because a repeatedly in-terrupted flow of action must necessarily have less force than an action directly carried through from its beginning to its conclu-sion. There may be exceptions to this general rule—we will con-sider that possibility later—but insofar as the general rule is persuasive it suggests that one of the chief mistakes a writer can make is to allow or force the reader's mind to be distracted, even momentarily, from the fictional dream.

Let us be sure we have the principle clear. The writer presents a scene—let us say a scene in which two rattlesnakes are locked in mortal combat. He makes the scene vivid in the reader's mind; that is, he encourages the reader to "dream" the event with enormous clarity, by presenting as many concrete details as possible. He shows, with as much poetic force as he can muster, how the heads hover, jaws wide, slowly swaying, and then strike; how the teeth sink in; how the tails switch and lash, grope for a hold, pound up dust clouds; how the two snakes hiss, occasionally strike and miss, the two rattles roaring like motors. By detail the writer achieves vividness; to make the scene continuous, he takes pains to avoid anything that might distract the reader from the image of fighting snakes to, say, the manner in which the image is presented or the character of the writer. This is of course not to say that the writer cannot break from the scene to some other—for instance, the conservationist rushing toward the snakes in his jeep. Though characters and locale change, the dream is still running like a movie in the reader's mind. The writer distracts the reader—breaks the film, if you will—when by some slip of technique or egoistic intrusion he allows or forces the reader to stop thinking about the story (stop "seeing" the story) and think about something else.

Some writers—John Barth, for instance—make a point of interrupting the fictional dream from time to time, or even denying the reader the chance to enter the fictional dream that his experience of fiction has led him to expect. We will briefly examine the purpose and value of such fiction later. For now, it is enough to say that such writers are not writing fiction at all, but something else, *metafiction.* They give the reader an experience that assumes the usual experience of fiction as its point of departure, and whatever effect their work may have depends on their conscious violation of the usual fictional effect. What interests us in their novels is that they are *not* novels but, instead, artistic comments on art.

We've come a long way from our opening question, "If there are no rules, or none worth his attention, where is the beginning writer to begin?" Among other things, you may impatiently object, we've raised the specter of a great morass of rules: Don't try to write without the basic skills of composition; don't try to write "what you know," choose a genre; create a kind of dream in the reader's mind, and avoid like the plague all that might briefly distract from that dream—a notion wherein a multitude of rules are implied.

But nothing in all this, I patiently answer, has anything to do with aesthetic law or gives rules on how to write. That literature falls into genres is simply an observation from nature, comparable to Adam's observation that the animals need names. If one is to write, it helps to know what writing is. And the fact that all three of the major genres have one common element, the fictional dream, is another observation, nothing more. We are speaking, remember, only of realistic narratives, tales, and yarns—that is, fiction's primary forms—so that in listing ways in which the reader can be distracted from the fictional dream, as I will in Part Two, I am in fact dealing only with things to watch out for when striving for the effects of traditional fiction. My premise of course is that before one can work well with metafiction, one needs some understanding of how the primary forms work.

Let us turn again, then, to that opening question: Where should one begin?

I have said that a good answer, but not an ideal one, is "Write the kind of story you know and like best"; in other words, choose a genre and try to write in it. Since we're living in an age very rich in genres—since a given student may have encountered almost anything, from tales like Isak Dinesen's to *New Yorker* realistic fiction, from surreal, plotless fictions-in-question-and-answer-form to philosophically enriched and dramatically intensified prose renderings of something like the vision in *Captain Marvel* comics—such instructions to the writer may produce almost anything. Set off in this way, the writer is sure to enjoy himself, first riffling through genres, discovering how many and how complex they are, then—tongue between his teeth—knocking off his brilliant example. The approach has the advantage of reminding the student of what freedom he has, how vast the possibilities are, and the advantage of encouraging him to find his own unique path.

The reason the approach seems to me not ideal is that, except in the extraordinary case, it wastes the writer's time. It instructs him to do something he cannot realistically be expected to do well—and here I mean "well" in the always urgent artist's sense, not the more casual, more gentlemanly way in which we do things badly or well in other university programs. Let me explain. True artists, whatever smiling faces they may show you, are obsessive, driven people—whether driven by some mania or driven by some high, noble vision need not presently concern us. Anyone who has worked both as artist and as professor can tell you, I think, that he works very differently in his two styles. No one is more careful, more scrupulously honest, more devoted to his personal vision of the ideal, than a good professor trying to write a book about the *Gilgamesh*. He may write far into the night, he may avoid parties, he may feel pangs of guilt about having spent too little time with his family. Nevertheless, his work is no more like an artist's work than the work of a first-class accountant is like that of an athlete contending for a championship. He uses faculties of the mind more easily available to us; he has, on all sides of him, stays, checks, safeties, rules of procedure that guide and secure him. He's a man sure of where he stands in the world. He belongs on sunlit walkways, in ivied halls. With the artist, not so. No critical study, however brilliant, is the fierce psychological battle a novel is. The qualities that make a true artist—nearly the same qualities that make a true athlete—make it important that the student writer never be prevented from working as seriously as he knows how to. In university courses we do exercises. Term papers, quizzes, final examinations are not meant for publication. We move through a course on Dostoevsky or Poe as we move through a mildly good cocktail party, picking up the good bits of food or conversation, bearing with the rest, going home when it comes to seem the reasonable thing to do. Art, at those moments when it feels most like art—when we feel most alive, most alert, most triumphant—is less like a cocktail party than a tank full of sharks. Everything's for keeps, nothing's just for exercise. (Robert Frost said, "I never write exercises, but sometimes I write poems which fail and then I call them exercises.") A course in creative writing should be like writing itself; everything required should be, at least potentially, usable, publishable: for keeps. "A *mighty will*," Henry James said, "that's all there is!" Let no one discourage or undermine that mighty will.

I would begin, then, with something real—smaller than a short story, tale, yarn, sketch—and something primary, not secondary (not parody, for example, but the thing itself). I would begin with some one of those necessary parts of larger forms, some single element that, if brilliantly done, might naturally become the trigger of a larger work—some small exercise in technique, if you like, as long as it's remembered that we do not really mean it as an exercise but mean it as a possible beginning of some magnificent work of art. A one-page passage of description, for example; description keyed to some particular genre—since description in a short story does not work in the same way description works in the traditional tale. And I would make the chief concern of this small exercise the writer's discovery of the *full meaning* of fiction's elements. Having written one superb descriptive passage, the writer should know things about description that he'll never need to think about again. Working element by element through the necessary parts of fiction, he should make the essential techniques second nature, so that he can use them with increasing dexterity and subtlety, until at last, as if effortlessly, he can construct imaginary worlds —huge thoughts made up of concrete details—so rich and complex, and so awesomely simple, that we are astounded, as we're always astounded by great art.

This means, of course, that he must learn to see fiction's elements as only a writer does, or an occasional great critic: as the fundamental units of an ancient but still valid kind of thought. Homer's kind of thought; what I have sometimes called "concrete philosophy." We're not ready just yet to talk about what that kind of thought entails, but we can make a beginning by describing how an exercise in description might work.

To the layman it may seem that description serves simply to tell us where things are happening, giving us perhaps some idea of what the characters are like by identifying them with their surroundings, or providing us with props that may later tip over or burn down or explode. Good description does far more: It is one of the writer's means of reaching down into his unconscious mind, finding clues to what questions his fiction must ask, and, with luck, hints about the answers. Good description is symbolic not because the writer plants symbols in it but because, by working in the proper way, he forces symbols still largely mysterious to him up into his conscious mind where, little by little as his fiction progresses, he can work with them and finally understand them. To put this another way, the organized and intelligent fictional dream that will eventually fill the reader's mind *begins as a largely mysterious dream in the writer's mind.* Through the process of writing and endless revising, the writer makes available the order the reader sees. Discovering the meaning and communicating the meaning are for the writer one single act. One does not simply describe a barn, then. One describes a barn as seen by someone in some particular mood, because only in that way can the barn—or the writer's experience of barns combined with whatever lies deepest in his feelings—be tricked into mumbling its secrets.

Consider the following as a possible exercise in description: Describe a barn as seen by a man whose son has just been killed in a war. Do not mention the son, or war, or death. Do not mention the man who does the seeing. (The exercise should run to about one typed page.) If the writer works hard, and if he has the talent to be a writer, the result of his work should be a powerful and disturbing image, a faithful description of some apparently real barn but one from which the reader gets a sense of the father's emotion; though exactly what that emotion is he may not be able to pin down. (In an actual piece of fiction, we would of course be told what the emotion is—telling important stories by sly implication is a species of frigidity. But knowing the emotion, we should get from the description no less powerful an effect.) No amount of *intellectual* study can determine for the writer what details he should include. If the description is to be effective, he must choose his boards, straw, pigeon manure, and ropes, the rhythms of his sentences, his angle of vision, by feeling and intuition. And one of the things he will discover, inevitably, is that the images of death and loss that come to him are not necessarily those we might expect. The hack mind leaps instantly to images of, for instance, darkness, heaviness, decay. But those may not be at all the kinds of images that drift into the mind that has emptied itself of all but the desire to "tell the truth"; that is, to get the feeling down in concrete details. In everything he writes—description, dialogue, the recounting of actions—the writer does the same thing. And so the writer gathers part—still only part—of the materials with which he does his thinking.

At this point the reader can no doubt guess what the remaining parts are. Obviously one does not think in exactly the same ways, or about exactly the same kinds of things, in a short story, a tale, and a yarn; and reflection on that fact leads to the further observation that, as Wallace Stevens put it, "a change of style is a change of subject." It was once a fairly common assumption among writers and literary critics that what fiction ought to do is tell the truth about things, or, as Poe says somewhere, express our intuitions of reality. Viewed in this way, fiction is a kind of instrument for coming to understanding. But we can see that there are problems to be solved if that view is to be defended. The realist says to us: "Show me, by a process of exact imitation, what it's like for a thirteen-year-old girl when she falls painfully, faintingly in love." And he folds his arms, smug in the conviction that *he* can do just that. But questions dismay us. Shall we tell the truth in short, clipped sentences or long, smooth, graceful ones? Shall we tell it using short vowels and hard consonants or long vowels and soft consonants?—because the choices we make may change everything. Does fiction, in fact, have anything whatever to do with truth? Is it possible that this complicated instrument, fiction, studies nothing but itself—its own processes?

A common answer at the present time is that that is the question the serious writer spends his whole life trying to work out by means of the only kind of thinking he trusts; that is, the fictional process. For the moment, we must let that answer stand —with only this reservation: Great fiction can make us laugh or cry, in much the way that life can, and it gives us at least the powerful illusion that when we do so we're doing pretty much the same things we do when we laugh at Uncle Herman's jokes, or cry at funerals. Somehow the endlessly recombining elements that make up works of fiction have their roots hooked, it seems, into the universe, or at least into the hearts of human beings. Somehow the fictional dream persuades us that it's a clear, sharp, edited version of the dream all around us. Whatever our doubts, we pick up books at train stations, or withdraw into our studies and write them; and the world—or so we imagine—comes alive.

3

Interest and Truth

Anything we read for pleasure we read because it interests us. One would think, since this is so, that the first question any young writer would ask himself, when he's trying to decide what to write, would be "What can I think of that's interesting?" Oddly enough, that is not a very usual first question; in fact, when one points out to young writers that it might be, they often react with surprise. To some extent, bad teaching is to blame, encouraging us to rise beyond, and forget, our most immediate, most childish pleasures—color in painting, melody in music, story in fiction—and learn to take pleasure in things more abstract and complex. Those sophisticated pleasures are real enough and can be intense, but something may have gone wrong when they come to be the first pleasures we seek. To read or write well, we must steer between two extreme views of aesthetic interest: the overemphasis of things immediately pleasurable (exciting plot, vivid characterization, fascinating atmosphere) and exclusive concern with that which is secondarily but at times more lastingly pleasurable, the fusing artistic vision.

Though it cannot be said of all teachers of literature, it is common to find teachers indifferent to the kinds of poetry and fiction that go most directly for those values we associate with simple entertainment—popular lyrics, drugstore paperbacks, and so forth. The reason may in some cases be snobbery, but probably just as often the cause is the sensitive reader's too frequent experience of disappointment—the boring sameness found at its extreme in the scripts of television Westerns, cop-shows, and situation comedies. Driven off by too much that is merely commercial—often shoddy imitation of authentic originality in the realm of the popular—we fail to notice that popular song writers like Stevie Wonder and Randy Newman, to say nothing of the Beatles, can be dedicated, energetic poets more interesting than many of the weary sophisticates, true-confessors, and randy academics we encounter in the "little magazines," and that drugstore fiction can often have more to offer than fiction thought to be of a higher class. The result of such prejudice or ignorance is that literature courses regularly feature writers less appealing—at least on the immediate, sensual level, but sometimes on deeper levels as well—than Isaac Asimov, Samuel R. Delaney, Walter M. Miller, Jr., Roger Zelazny, or the Strugatsky brothers, science-fiction writers; or even thriller writers like John le Carré and Frederick Forsyth; the creators of the early *Spider-Man* comics or *Howard the Duck*. In theory it may be proper that teachers ignore thrillers, science fiction, and the comic books. No one wants Coleridge pushed from the curriculum by a duck "trapped in a world he never made!" But when we begin to list the contemporary "serious" writers who fill highschool and literature courses, *Howard the Duck* can look not all that bad.

The snobbery or limited range of teachers is one of the reasons we forget to think about interest in the sense of immediate appeal; but another cause may be more basic. The business of education is to give the student both useful information and life-enhancing experience, one largely measurable, the other not; and since the life-enhancing value of a course in literature is difficult to measure—since, moreover, many people in a position to put pressure on educational programs have no real experience in or feeling for the arts—it is often tempting to treat life-enhancement courses as courses in useful information, putting them on the same "objective" level as courses in civics, geometry, or elementary physics. So it comes about that books are taught (officially, at least) not because they give joy, the incomparably rich experience we ask and expect of all true art, but because, as a curriculum committee might put it, they "illustrate major themes in American literature," or "present a clearly stated point of view and can thus serve as a vehicle for such curriculum objectives as (1) demonstrating an awareness of the author's purpose, (2) reading critically, and (3) identifying organizational patterns in literary selections used to support a point of view." One cannot exactly say that such teaching is pernicious, but to treat great works of literature in this way seems a little like arguing for preservation of dolphins, whales, chimps, and gorillas solely on the grounds of ecological balance.

At all levels, not just in the highschools (as the above might suggest), novels, short stories, and poems have for years been taught not as experiences that can delight and enliven the soul but as things that are good for us, like vitamin C. The whole idea of the close critical analysis of literary works—the idea emphasized by the "New Critics" of the thirties and forties—has had the accidental side effect of leading to the notion that the chief virtue of good poetry and fiction is instructional. If we look at the famous New Critical anthologies designed to teach analysis (for instance, *Understanding Fiction* and *Understanding Poetry*, by Cleanth Brooks and Robert Penn Warren), we cannot help noticing that subtly, no doubt unwittingly, the authors suggest that what makes a piece of literature "good" is the writer's thorough and orderly exploration of ideas, his full development of the implications of his theme. What these authors suggest is in important ways true, though ill-considered books "against interpretation" (as one of them is entitled) have driven close analysis from many classrooms: However dazzling and vivid the characters, however startling the action, no piece of fiction can be of lasting interest if its thought is confused, simple-minded, or plain wrong. On the other hand, reading fiction or poetry without regard for the delight it can give—its immediate interest—can mutilate the experience of reading. It is not incidental that Shakespeare's plays present fascinating characters engaged in suspenseful actions. To write fiction without regard for immediate interest, purposely choosing the most colorless characters possible, a plot calculated to drive away the poor slob interested in seeing something happen, and suppressing all textural richness and variety—to write, that is, as if fiction were much too serious to be enjoyed—is to raise suspicion that the writer is as insensitive to art's true nature, and its value to humanity, as a stone in a farmer's field.

But what gives a work of fiction aesthetic interest? For the moment let us ignore fiction's flashy young cousin metafiction, since much of what we say here we must take back when we turn to metafiction.

Nothing in the world is inherently interesting—that is, immediately interesting, and interesting in the same degree, to all human beings. And nothing can be made to be of interest to the reader that was not first of vital concern to the writer. Each writer's prejudices, tastes, background, and experience tend to limit the kinds of characters, actions, and settings he can honestly care about, since by the nature of our mortality we care about what we know and might possibly lose (or have already lost), dislike that which threatens what we care about, and feel indifferent toward that which has no visible bearing on our safety or the safety of the people and things we love. Thus no two writers get aesthetic interest from exactly the same materials. Mark Twain, saddled with a cast of characters selected by Henry James, would be quick to maneuver them all into wells. Yet all writers, given adequate technique—technique that communicates—can stir our interest in their special subject matter, since at heart all fiction treats, directly or indirectly, the same thing: our love for people and the world, our aspirations and fears. The particular characters, actions, and settings are merely instances, variations on the universal theme.

If this is so—it may be useful to notice in passing—then the writer who denies that human beings have free will (the writer who really denies it, not jokingly or ironically pretends to deny it) is one who can write nothing of interest. Aside from a grotesquery that must soon grow repetitious, he cannot endow characters, places, and events with real interest because he can find no real interest in them in the first place. Stripped of free will—robbed of all capacity to fight for those things they aspire to and avoid those things they fear—human beings cease to be of anything more than scientific and sentimental interest. For the writer who views his characters as helpless biological organisms, mere units in a mindless social structure, or cogs in a mechanistic universe, whatever values those characters may hold must necessarily be illusions, since none of the characters can do anything about them, and the usual interplay of value against value that makes for an interesting exploration of theme must here be a cynical and academic exercise.

If it is true that no two writers get aesthetic interest from exactly the same materials, yet true that all writers, given adequate technique, can stir our interest in their special subject matter—since all human beings have the same root experience (we're born, we suffer, we die, to put it grimly), so that all we need for our sympathy to be roused is that the writer communicate with power and conviction the similarities in his characters' experience and our own—then it must follow that the first business of the writer must be to make us see and feel vividly what his characters see and feel. However odd, however wildly unfamiliar the fictional world—odd as hog-farming to a fourth-generation Parisian designer, or Wall Street to an unemployed tuba player—we must be drawn into the characters' world as if we were born to it.

To say this is to take, admittedly, an extreme position. There are limits to the extent to which people of one culture can imaginatively embrace the experience of people from another, and a more cautious statement of the argument I'm offering would be that the writer should make his characters' world sensually available to a wide range of readers, knowing in advance that for many readers (Tibetans, perhaps), his characters' experience will be beyond comprehension. Some writers offer a still narrower view, that it's sufficient to make one's characters' experience vivid for only that small group of readers whose background is similar to that of the characters. Only a writer from some great cultural center like Paris or New York can afford such a position. The man from Wyoming, if he cannot communicate his experience to New York, is unlikely to get published. So the writer who limits his audience so narrowly is likely to seem parochial, if not arrogant, to those readers not born in his city or desperate to improve their status by seeming to have lived there. But every writer must make his own choice.

The basic principle stands in any case, at least so long as fiction contains characters at all: The writer must enable us to see and feel vividly what his characters see and feel; that is, enable us to experience as directly and intensely as possible, though vicariously, what his characters experience. How can the writer best do this?

Some of the answer should by now be obvious. The writer must of necessity write in a style that falls somewhere on the continuum running from objective to subjective; in other words, from the discursive, essayist's style, in which everything is spelled out as scientifically as possible, to the poetic style, in which nothing (or practically nothing) is explained, everything is evoked, or, to use Henry James' term, "rendered." The essayist's style is by nature slow-moving and laborious, more wide than deep. It tends toward abstraction and precision without much power, as we see instantly when we compare any two descriptions, one discursive, one poetic. In the essayist's style we might write, for instance, "The man in the doorway was large and apparently ill at ease—so large that he had to stoop a little and draw in his elbows." The poetic style can run harder at its effects: "He filled the doorway, awkward as a horse." Both styles, needless to say, can be of use. One builds its world up slowly and completely, as Tolstoy does in *Anna Karenina*, where very few metaphors or similes appear; the other lights up its imaginary world by lightning flashes. In contemporary fiction the essayist's style is to some extent out of fashion at the moment, or, rather, is used almost exclusively for purposes of irony and humor, since its labored pace can easily be made to reflect pompousness or ennui. But literary fashion never need be taken very seriously. Styles are born in human attitudes, and since Homer's time the total range of possible human attitudes has probably not changed much.

Wherever the writer's style falls on the continuum running from objective to subjective, what counts in conventional fiction must be the vividness and continuity of the fictional dream the words set off in the reader's mind. The writer's characters must stand before us with a wonderful clarity, such continuous clarity that nothing they do strikes us as improbable behavior for just that character, even when the character's action is, as sometimes happens, something that came as a surprise to the writer himself. We must understand, and the writer before us must understand, more than we *know* about the character; otherwise neither the writer nor the reader after him could feel confident of the character's behavior when the character acts freely. So it is that Trollope discovers to his astonishment, or so he tells us, that Mrs. Eustace stole her own diamonds. Though her action was not in his original plan, his deep, intuitive knowledge of the character, developed over time, tells him instantly, the moment he gets his first clue, that the act is indeed one that would flow inevitably and surely out of her being. How is this possible? How can a writer—and after him the reader—have this sure knowledge of some personality that literally does not exist?

Begin with the crucial observation here that, except as creatures of the imagination, characters in fiction do not exist. It is true that Mrs. Eustace may be based on, say, Trollope's Aunt Maude. But except in the writing of a biography (and, strictly speaking, not even there), a writer cannot take a character from life. Every slightest change the writer makes in the character's background and experience must have subtle repercussions. I am not the same person I would have been if my father had been rich, or had owned elephants. Trollope's Aunt Maude can no longer remain perfectly herself once she's married to Mr. Eustace. Subtle details change characters' lives in ways too complex for the conscious mind to grasp, though we nevertheless grasp them. Thus plot not only changes but creates character: By our actions we discover what we really believe and, simultaneously, reveal ourselves to others. And setting influences both character and plot: One cannot do in a thunderstorm what one does on a hot day in Jordan. (One's camel slips, or, from homesickness, refuses to budge; so the assassin goes uncaught, the President is shot, the world is again plunged into war.) As in the universe every atom has an effect, however minuscule, on every other atom, so that to pinch the fabric of Time and Space at any point is to shake the whole length and breadth of it, so in fiction every element has effect on every other, so that to change a character's name from Jane to Cynthia is to make the fictional ground shudder under her feet.

Thus it appears that to make us see and feel vividly what his characters see and feel—to draw us into the characters' world as if we were born to it—the writer must do more than simply make up characters and then somehow explain and authenticate them (giving them the right kinds of motorcycles and beards, exactly the right memories and jargon). He must shape simultaneously (in an expanding creative moment) his characters, plot, and setting, each inextricably connected to the others; he must make his whole world in a single, coherent gesture, as a potter makes a pot; or, as Coleridge puts it, he must copy, with his finite mind, the process of the infinite "I AM."

We are now in a position to look at the problem of aesthetic interest in a new light. First, and least important, we're in a position to give tentative answers to those "innovative fictionists," as they call themselves, who feel impatient with traditional expectations of character and plot. Character, these writers sometimes claim, is a part of the traditional novel's unnecessary baggage and ought to be discarded. The novel, they argue—and they would say the same of shorter kinds of fiction—once served purposes we can now perceive to be nonessential to its nature. For instance, in an age when travel was travail, when photographs and movies were not yet invented, and sociological studies were unheard of, it was the novelist who told us what life was like in Venice or New Orleans. He described the architecture, climate, and vegetation, told us of the history and sociology of the place; in short, made us feel as if we'd been there. Now we can go there, or get specialized books and picture postcards. Similarly the novelist told us about character, relating people's attitudes and actions to the customs and climate from which they spring, or delving into the mysteries now demystified by psychology and neurology. By the old, now outmoded theory, they explain, fiction was a means of discovering or revealing how things happen in the world. We read of a woman in Chicago who threw her father out the window of her sixth-floor apartment. "How in the world could such a terrible thing have come about?" we exclaim, and the novelist's business is to show us, step by step, what happened. That theory of fiction was exploded the day Poe wrote "The Cask of Amontillado," a story that has an end but no beginning or middle; hence its success is a flat refutation of Aristotle's theory that what is central to fiction is *energeia*; that is, "the actualization of the potential which exists in character and situation." Poe frees Kafka to write: "One day Gregor Samsa awoke to discover that he had been changed into a large cockroach." Who knows how or why? Who cares? By the selection and arrangement of the materials of his fiction, the writer gives us not the truth about the world and how things come about but an image of himself, "a portrait of the artist"—or perhaps nothing more than an interesting construction, an object for our study and amusement.

This view, now common, has important virtues. It encourages the writer to think in new ways, broadening the fictional experience. If Lois Lane and Superman were to wander into a scene by Henry James, what would they think of it and how would they affect it? The answer does not matter—it cannot properly be called correct or incorrect—it is merely interesting. If the state of California were to sink into the sea, how would daily life be changed in Brooklyn? Again, if plot is no longer important (since its justification and central interest is its revelation of the potential in character and situation), why should fiction have profluence—our sense, as we read, that we're "getting somewhere"? If the portrait of the artist is all that really counts, why not an artist who simply chats with us, plays with us, perhaps even insults us, creating not an action we can follow to its end but a small, highly flavored imitation of Eternity? The longer we think along these lines, the more interesting the aesthetic possibilities become. If the artist's revelation of himself is his style—not just his style in choosing words and phrases, sentence rhythms and ways of building paragraphs (or destroying the whole idea of the phrase, the sentence, the paragraph), but also his style in choosing details from reality or dream; elements, that is, of character and setting—what happens, in terms of aesthetic interest, if the writer offers not his own materials but someone else's? Thus Borges gives us the image of a brilliant modern writer whose great opus is, word for word, Cervantes' *Don Quixote*, and Donald Barthelme, in his short story "Paraguay," borrows (and footnotes) a landscape description that in fact has to do not with Paraguay but with Tibet.

These are of course the arguments raised against conventional fiction by people more interested in metafiction. None of the arguments against conventional fiction will hold, and looking closely at conventional fiction's defense will help us see clearly what the interest and "truth" in conventional fiction are.

Once we have fiction's nature clear, we can better appreciate the special interest of metafiction, a subject to which we will turn in the next chapter.

The traditionalist answer to the "innovative fictionist's" general line of argument might go like this: Innovative fictions of the kind just discussed are not inherently wrong-headed, merely unserious. Whatever interest or value they have they derive from their contrast with "traditional"—that is, "conventional" or "normal"—fiction. So long as conventional fiction remains adequate and worthwhile, innovative fictions are literary stunts. They have a kind of interest, as intellectual toys, but they engage us only for the moment. Though traditional serious fiction may also be play, since it deeply involves us with the troubles of characters who do not in fact exist, the play in serious traditional fiction bears on life, not just art. As we play at compassion, weeping for Little Nell or Ophelia, we exercise faculties we know to be vitally important in real life. If the assembly of made-up materials in a fiction creates a portrait of the artist, the importance of the portrait is not that it tells us what the artist looks like but that it provides us with a focus, an aperture, a medium (as in a séance) for seeing things beyond and more important than the artist. In the artist's recreation of the world we are enabled to see the world. Granted, no two artists reveal to us exactly the same world, just as no two windows do; and granted, moreover, since artists are human and therefore limited, some dedicated and serious artists may be windows smudged by dirt, others may distort like blistered and warped panes, still others may be stained glass. But the world they frame is the world that is really out there (or in here: Insofar as human nature is everywhere the same, it makes no difference). A powerful part of our interest as we read great literature is our sense that we're "onto something." And part of our boredom when we read books in which the vision of life seems paltry-minded is our sense that we are not.

Aristotle's idea of the energeic action is not really refuted by

Poe's "Cask of Amontillado" or Kafka's "Metamorphosis," though those works may lead us to understand the theory in a new way, a way Aristotle never thought of, working as he did from the practice of Greek tragedians, but one to which he might without too great an effort adapt himself. Poe and Kafka begin not with exterior situations whose potential is to be actualized in the progress of the work, but with situations that are, in one case literally and in the other expressionistically, interior. Whereas Sophocles' initial situation in *Oedipus Rex* is a plague in Thebes and the king's dark history, as yet unknown to the king himself, Poe's initial situation is almost entirely a psychological state, the central character's hunger for revenge (whether or not the hunger is even justified the reader cannot tell), and Kafka's initial situation is a psychological state expressionistically transformed: Where the realist would say, "One day Gregor Samsa woke up to the realization that he was like a cockroach," the expressionist heightens or intensifies reality by turning the metaphor to fact. In place of the classical writer's clear distinction between the outside world and the inside world—"situation," on one hand, "character," on the other—the two modern writers see outer reality and inner reality as interpenetrating: The world is whatever we feel it to be, so that the situation character must deal with is partly character. Either way, the unfolding of the story is the actualization of its initial potential.

Two central tenets, for the traditional point of view, are, first, the Coleridgian notion that true literary art is "the repetition in the finite mind of the infinite 'I AM' "—the idea, that is, that, like God opening his fist, the writer creates everything at once, his characters, their actions, and their world, each element dependent on the others—and, second, the concomitant notion that an important part of what interests us in good fiction is our sense, as we read, that the writer's imitation of reality's process ("the ineluctable modality of the visible," as Stephen Dedalus puts it) is accurate; that is, our feeling that the work, even if it contains fabulous elements, is in some deep way "true to life." The obvious question is: How can the writer possibly do so much at once?

The answer is that he does and he doesn't. He can think, consciously, of only a few things at a time; but the process by which he works eventually leads him to his goal. To anyone who thinks about it carefully, this must at first seem a rather strange statement: "The process by which he works eventually leads him to his goal"—as if the process had some kind of magic in it, some daemonic will of its own. Indeed, some writers—not the least of them Homer—have taken that point of view, speaking without apology of Muses as, in some sense, actual beings, and of "epic song" and "memory" (not quite in our sense) as forces greater than and separate from the poet. We often hear even modern writers speak of their work as somehow outside their control, informed by a spirit that, when they read their writing later, they cannot identify as having come from themselves. I imagine every good writer has had this experience. It testifies to the remarkable subtlety of fiction as a mode of thought.

The fictional process is the writer's way of thinking, a special case of the symbolic process by means of which we do all our thinking. Though it's only an analogy, and in some ways misleading, we might say that the elements of fiction are to a writer what numbers are to a mathematician, the main difference being that we handle fictional elements more intuitively than even the subtlest mathematicians handle numbers. As Hobbes said, "We cannot think about things but only about the names of things"; in other words, to build up a complicated argument we need abstractions. If we wish to think usefully about wildlife preservation, we must abstract the dying white rhinoceros at our feet to dying white rhinoceroses in general, we must see the relationship (another abstraction) between dying white rhinoceroses and dying tigers, etc., and rise, finally, to the abstraction "dying wildlife." In the same way, a writer consciously or unconsciously abstracts the elements of fiction.

By the elements of fiction I mean all of the discrete particles of which a story is built, particles that might be removed, undamaged, from one story and placed in another; for example, particles of the action, "event ideas" such as kidnapping, pursuit of the elusive loved one, a murder, loss of identity, and so on; or particles that go to make up character, such as obesity and each of the things obesity may imply, or stinginess, or lethargy; or particles that go to make up setting and atmosphere. In isolation, each element has relatively limited meaning; in juxtaposition to one another, the elements become more significant, forming abstractions of a kind—higher units of poetic thought. All the arts are made up of such fundamental elements, which we find repeated in painting after painting, symphony after symphony, arranged and built up (as complex molecules are built up from atoms) in an infinite variety of ways. From painting we might take the example of the mountain (one element) and the tree (another) that in juxtaposition have a standard but variable function: The majestic mountain is silhouetted against the sky and compared to a single, equally isolated tree in the foreground, the one remote, unchanging, and divine in connotation, the other accessible, ever-changing, and humanized. We find this juxtaposition of elements expressed in its classical form in Titian, Poussin, and other masters; in several of the late works of Cézanne—the Mont-Sainte-Victoire paintings of 1902–1906 —we find the traditional juxtaposition ingeniously varied, the tree mysteriously dominating the mountain and treated in such a way (swirling brushstrokes, vague outlines) that it seems at least as mystical as the mountain; or the tree and the mountain so identified, by color and frantic brushstrokes, that the accessible and the remote, or human emotion and the ideal, seem to merge; and so forth.

Though no one can say what the number is, the number of fictional elements that exist is finite, like the number of words in the English language. Like the tree and the mountain in our example from painting, or like words in the English language, the elements of fiction may mean one thing in one place, another in another; they slip and slide and occasionally overlap; but they have meaning—or, at any rate, meaning domains—and so do their standard, increasingly complex juxtapositions. Good writers use them as skillfully and comfortably, and sometimes as unconsciously, as plumbers and roofers use language. No new elements are likely to be discovered; this is what we mean, or ought to mean, when we say that "literature is exhausted." What writers do discover is new combinations. The search for new combinations is both guided by and one with the fictional process.

Perhaps the logical first step in the fictional process is the writer's conscious or intuitive recognition of the nature of narrative, and his acceptance of the shackles imposed by his decision to tell a story (instead of, say, to write a philosophy book or paint a picture). By definition—and of aesthetic necessity—a story contains profluence, a requirement best satisfied by a sequence of causally related events, a sequence that can end in only one of two ways: in resolution, when no further event can take place (the murderer has been caught and hanged, the diamond has been found and restored to its owner, the elusive lady has been captured and married), or in logical exhaustion, our recognition that we've reached the stage of infinite repetition; more events might follow, perhaps from now till Kingdom Come, but they will all express the same thing—for example, the character's entrapment in empty ritual or some consistently wrong response to the pressures of his environment. Resolution is of course the classical and usually more satisfying conclusion; logical exhaustion satisfies us intellectually but often not emotionally, since it's more pleasing to see things definitely achieved or thwarted than to be shown why they can never be either achieved or thwarted. Both achievement and failure give importance to the thing sought; we can feel about it as we feel about values. Logical exhaustion usually reveals that the character's supposed exercise of free will was illusory.

It might be objected here that no law requires art to be "pleasing." A story that raises expectations, then shows why they can neither be satisfied nor denied, can be as illuminating, and as interesting moment by moment, as any other kind of story, though the ending may annoy us. The trouble, from the traditionalist point of view, is this. First, the revelation that the character's exercise of free will was illusory raises suspicions, which may or may not be justified, about the author's honesty and artistic responsibility. It may be that the writer was as surprised and disappointed by the inescapable conclusion to his fictional argument as we have been; yet we cannot help wondering how much real interest he felt from the beginning in his characters and events: The conclusion suggests that he has used them rather than cared about them, much as a preacher uses old stories and straw men to drive home some point. In rousing our concern about the characters and events—such is our suspicion, right or wrong—he has set us up, treating us not as equals but as poor dumb mules who must be hollered and whipped into wisdom. Second, we suspect the writer of a kind of frigidity. By the nature of our mortality, I pointed out earlier, we care about what we know and might possibly lose, dislike that which threatens what we care about, and feel indifferent toward that which has no visible bearing on our safety or the safety of what we love. Though we do not read fiction primarily in order to find rules on how to live or, indeed, to find anything that is directly useful, we do sympathetically engage ourselves in the struggle that produces the fictional events. Reading a piece of fiction that ends up nowhere—no win, no loss; life as a treadmill —is like discovering, after we have run our hearts out against the timekeeper's clock, that the timekeeper forgot to switch the clock on. The only emotions such fiction can ordinarily produce are weariness and despair, and those emotions, though valid and perhaps even justified (finally) by the nature of the universe, are less useful to the conduct of our lives than are the emotions we exercise in other kinds of fiction. Not even Aristotle would argue that fiction *ought* to be cathartic; he says only that such fiction is most satisfying. But certainly more is involved than simple pleasure or displeasure. At least in comparison with the resolved ending (Aristotle would have said if the question had come up), the ending in logical exhaustion is morally repugnant.

We have said that by definition and aesthetic necessity a story contains profluence, and that the conventional kind of profluence—though other kinds are possible—is a causally related sequence of events. This is the root interest of all conventional narrative. Because he is intellectually and emotionally involved—that is, interested—the reader is led by successive, seemingly inevitable steps, with no false steps, and no necessary steps missing, from an unstable initial situation to its relatively stable outcome. It seems a pity that it should be necessary to argue a point so obvious, and I will not, at any length; to instruct the reader that he should quit when he gets bored, or instruct the writer that he should try not to be boring, seems absurd. Nevertheless, current fictional theory and the practice of some fashionable writers make at least some discussion of the matter worthwhile.

A basic characteristic of all good art, then—all man-made works that are aesthetically interesting and lasting is a concord of ends and means, or form and function. The *sine qua non* of narrative, so far as form is concerned, is that it takes time. We cannot read a whole novel in an instant, so to be coherent, to work as a unified experience necessarily and not just accidentally temporal, narrative must show some profluence of development. What the logical progress of an argument is to nonfiction, event-sequence is to fiction. Page 1, even if it's a page of description, raises questions, suspicions, and expectations; the mind casts forward to later pages, wondering what will come about and how. It is this casting forward that draws us from paragraph to paragraph and chapter to chapter. At least in conventional fiction, the moment we stop caring where the story will go next, the writer has failed, and we stop reading. The shorter the fiction, needless to say, the less the need for plot profluence. A story of three or four pages may still interest though it has practically no movement. And of course not all fiction need move at the same pace. Runners of the hundred-yard dash do not take off in the same way runners of the marathon do. If the opening pages of a thousand-page novel would serve equally well as the opening pages of a short story, the likelihood is that the novel-opening is wrong. (This is not quite a firm rule, admittedly. A long novel may begin with great urgency, then gradually settle into its long-distance stride. But the writer's timing in his opening pages is a signal to his reader's expectations.)

In any case, any narrative more than a few pages long is doomed to failure if it does not set up and satisfy plot expectations. Plotting, then—however childish and elementary it may seem in comparison with the work of surgeons, philosophers, or nuclear physicists—must be the first and foremost concern of the writer. He cannot work out his sequence of events without at least some notion of who the characters are to be or where the action is to take place, and in practice he will never design a plot without some notion of what its elements imply. To say that plot must be the writer's first concern is not to say that it is necessarily the first thing that dawns on him, setting off his project. The writer's first idea for the story—what Henry James calls the "germ"—may not be an event but an interesting character, setting, or theme. But whatever the origin of the story idea, the writer has no story until he has figured out a plot that will efficiently and elegantly express it. Though character is the emotional core of great fiction, and though action with no meaning beyond its own brute existence can have no lasting appeal, plot is—or must sooner or later become—the focus of every good writer's plan.

The writer works out plot in one of three ways: by borrowing some traditional plot or an action from real life (the method of the Greek tragedians, Shakespeare, Dostoevsky, and many other writers, ancient and modern); by working his way back from his story's climax; or by groping his way forward from an initial situation. Since usually one does not work out plot all at once, but broods over it, mentally trying alternatives, taking notes, carrying the idea in the back of one's mind as one reads or does one's laundry, working and reworking it for days or months or, sometimes, years, one may in practice work both backward and forward or even in all three of the possible ways simultaneously. Whatever happens in life—a curious fact one comes across in one's reading (why it is that pit vipers can see in the dark), a snatch of conversation, something from the newspapers, a fight with one's landlord—all this becomes possible material for the shaping of the plot, or for characters, setting, and theme as they may influence the plot. In a later chapter ("Plotting"), we will examine in detail how by each of the three methods I've mentioned above—and by other methods less likely to produce art—the writer builds up his story. For the moment, more general observations and an abstract analysis of just one kind of plotting will serve.

The writer who begins with a traditional story or some action drawn from life has part of his work done for him already. He knows what happened and, in general, why. The main work left to him is that of figuring out what part of the story (if not the whole) he wants to tell, what the most efficient way of telling it is, and why it is that it interests him.

Say the story that has caught his attention is that of Helen of Troy. The myth is large and complex and comes down to us in many forms, some of them contradictory, if not mutually exclusive, some versions strictly fabulous—as when Helen's mother, Leda, is raped by Zeus in the guise of a swan, or as when Paris stands before the three goddesses, attempting to choose between them—other versions suitable for modern realistic treatment. A given writer may find his interest stirred by almost any of the story's main events. Troy was a rich, cosmopolitan city; in its ruins, archeologists found jade, among other things, proving that Trojan traders had contacts as far away as China. The Achaians, on the other hand, whom Helen left when she fled from her husband with her Trojan lover, Paris, were cowherds, goatherds, raiders—from the Trojan point of view crude barbarians. How surprised Helen must have been, to say nothing of how Paris and his father the king felt, when her people dropped everything, called together relatives from far and wide, left their lean-tos and harsh, stone towns, and came after her with a thousand ships. That moment, her alarm at the news, might make a story. Again, when the Achaians pulled their famous trick, the peace-offering of the Trojan horse, which the Trojans dragged inside the walls of the city, unaware that it was loaded with Achaian soldiers, Helen is said to have gone out at night and to have called to the soldiers in the voices of their wives, hoping she could trick them into revealing themselves—but she said nothing to the Trojans of her suspicions. That event, too, has a strangeness that might make a good story.

The writer may decide to treat both of these events, perhaps others as well, in a single work; but to the extent that each event forms a narrative climax, he thinks out the two or more events as separate narrative units, or episodes. For each episode's climactic event, he borrows from legend or makes up on his own exactly as much as he needs in order to make the climactic event (a) meaningful and (b) convincing. For instance: If we are (a) fully to understand Helen's surprise at the arrival of her relatives (if the event is in this primary sense to have meaning; never mind the larger philosophical implications), and if we're (b) to be convinced that her relatives really did come in such astounding numbers, the writer must somehow find a way to show us clearly (1) what these strange people the Achaians are like that they'd react in such a way, (2) what the Trojans are like, and especially Paris, that he should make such a blunder, and (3) why Helen did not anticipate her kinsmen's response. All this, if the story is to be vivid and suspenseful, the writer must find a way to show us dramatically, by enacted scenes, not authorial essays or lengthy set speeches by the characters. If the story is to be efficient and elegant (in the sense that mathematical proofs are elegant), the writer must introduce no more background events or major characters than strictly necessary (and, obviously, no less), and must introduce these materials in the smallest possible number of scenes, each scene rhythmically proportionate to those surrounding, so that the pace is regular or, if appropriate, in regular acceleration. In other words, if it is possible to show in a single scene—clearly and powerfully— both what the Achaians are like and why Helen will not anticipate their response to her flight with Paris, the efficient and elegant writer does not use two or three scenes. By *scene* we mean here all that is included in an unbroken flow of action from one incident in time to another (the scene at the breakfast table, the scene out by the chariot two hours later, the scene between Helen and the priest in the temple, or whatever). The action within a scene is "unbroken" in the sense that it does not include a major time lapse or a leap from one setting to another —though the characters may, of course, walk or ride from one place to another without breaking the scene, the camera, so to speak, dollying after them. The action within a scene need *not* be "unbroken" in the sense that it includes no flashbacks or brief authorial interruptions for background explanation. The scene is not broken, in other words, when a character's mind drifts from present surrounding to some earlier scene, which is then vividly set before us for the time the flashback lasts. The efficient and elegant writer makes each scene bear as much as it can without clutter or crowding, and moves by the smoothest, swiftest transitions possible from scene to scene.

In addition to watching the rhythm of his scene—the tempo or pace—the writer pays close attention, in constructing the scene, to the relationship, in each of its elements, of emphasis and function. By emphasis we mean the amount of time spent on a particular detail; by function we mean the work done by that detail within the scene and the story as a whole. Let us say that at some point Helen steps behind a curtain to look for a lost brooch, and because she is there she happens to overhear a conversation. Since the function of Helen's stepping behind the curtain is relatively slight and mechanical, the good writer gets her behind the curtain as quickly as possible (having set up the lost brooch earlier, so that her action seems inevitable and natural). If he dwells at length on the appearance of the curtain, or Helen's gesture as she steps in behind it, the moment's emphasis is disproportionate to its function and becomes a dull spot in the narrative, or annoyingly misleading since the author's hoo-rah about Helen's disappearance leads us to expect some larger outcome than we get.

All these considerations the author bears in mind, consciously or intuitively, as he constructs his sequence of events leading to the climax (Helen's surprise). If his story plan is to be successful, he must rightly analyze what is logically necessary to the climax. If he shows us what the Achaians are like and what the Trojans are like, but fails to realize that he must also show us why Helen does not guess how her kinsmen will behave, the climax will lack inevitability and, therefore, power. Again, if the plan of the story is to work, the writer's solutions to the problems involved in authenticating the climax must be credible and apt. If Helen loses her brooch by throwing it at her husband, Menelaos, partly because Menelaos is a drunkard and a lazy oaf and partly because, against her will, she's falling in love with their guest Paris and his fine city ways, the curtain scene may be conveniently explained, but we are likely to doubt that Menelaos, even with the help of his brother Agamemnon, could organize the huge, stern-minded force that goes after her. Thus in thinking about plot, the writer must also think about character and its effects.

He must think, at the same time, about why it is that the story interests him. Whether he is using a traditional plot, an action drawn from life, or something he's made up, no writer chooses his story by pure whim or the mechanical combination of random elements. For the good writer, nothing is easier than making up possible stories. If pushed, he can spin them out hour after hour, each one of them theoretically sound—a sequence of events leading to some climax, or, in longer narratives, an episodic sequence of climaxes. (Helen's surprise and helplessness might naturally lead to a second climax, her behavior below the Trojan horse.) But of the thirty plots he can think up in an hour, only one—if even that—will catch and hold his interest, make him want to write. How odd, a different writer might say, that of all the stories one might tell about Helen, this writer has chosen a trivial, psychological climax, Helen's surprise! What the writer's interest means is that the climactic event has struck some chord in him, one that seems worth exploration. It's by the whole process of first planning the fiction and then writing it— elaborating characters and details of setting, finding the style that seems appropriate to the feeling, discovering unanticipated requirements of the plot—that the writer finds out and communicates the story's significance, intuited at the start. He knows that his first job is to authenticate what I earlier called the story's *primary* meaning: Helen's surprise. The surprise is a feeling, one that strikes us as conclusive, an implied discovery. But, like all conclusive feelings, Helen's surprise suggests some larger, *secondary* meaning, not just one person's feeling but a universal human feeling, some affirmation or recognition of a value. It is usually in this larger, secondary sense that we speak of the "meaning" of works of art.

The larger "meaning" of a story, we should pause here to note, may or may not come from our abstraction of or thought about what I've called above a conclusive emotion. But it does always come (at least this is true in every case I can think of) from feeling. In the classic case—as in the Helen story we're in the process of making up—it comes with the resolution of irony; that is, it comes at the moment the character knows what we know and have known for some time. *King Lear. Emma. Middlemarch.* In our Helen story, if the writer has done his work well, *we* know what the Achaians are like and what the Trojans are like, how the Achaian community, though at first glance crude and barbaric, has a profound sense of kin responsibility, a sense of justice and propriety that it is willing to extend even to invited guests (Paris, when he goes to Menelaos' house and first meets Helen), and how the Trojan community, though vastly superior in its culture and sophistication, superior, too, in its cosmopolitan evolution beyond ethnocentricity, has become morally lax and has perhaps come to expect a similar moral laxity in others (so that Paris does not anticipate the Achaian response); but though *we* know all this, Helen, because something has distracted her attention—a point we must return to—does not know until word comes that the Achaian ships have been sighted. In other kinds of story, the secondary or larger meaning may be released in other ways. For example, it may be our feeling about the whole movement of the story, not the final emotion of the character, that we abstract to an affirmation of values (secondary meaning). In the naturalist mode—fiction like Dreiser's—the character fights ferociously for something but is finally beaten down by overwhelming forces and ends in sorrow or despair, not fully aware of what has happened to him. It is not the despair that we abstract to some universal value, but the struggle. But however it may be achieved, in all great fiction, primary emotion (our emotion as we read, or the characters' emotions, or some combination of both) must sooner or later lift off from the particular and be transformed to an expression of what is universally good in human life—what promotes happiness for the individual alone and in society; in other words, some statement on value. In good fiction, this universal statement is likely to be too subtle, too loaded with qualifications, to be expressed in any way but the story's way; it may be impossible, that is, to reduce to any rule of behavior or general thesis. We *understand* the value, understand it with great precision, but even the shrewdest literary critic may have trouble formulating it in words and thus telling us the story's "message."

It is in this sense that the "philosophy" in fiction is "concrete philosophy": Fiction's meaning (what I have called secondary meaning) is as substantial, or grounded in the actual, as are the elements of which it is built. So it is that Aristotle tells us that a dramatic action, like life, can imply the metaphysical, so that as the philosopher abstracts from the actual to metaphysical theory, the literary critic or sensitive reader can abstract out the metaphysical implications of fictional events; but fiction's meaning can no more become, by itself, metaphysical than a cow in a field can evolve into a Platonic idea.

Perhaps an analogy may be of help here. In orthodox Christianity the believer is told that all formal codes, even the shifting codes of situational ethics, are supplanted by "the person of Christ." "I am the Way," Christ says, meaning, by one standard interpretation, that if the believer will give up his heart and soul to Christ, letting Christ's personality "enter in" like a daemonic force, he can then act rightly in every situation, because in fact he is no longer the agent; Christ is—a divinity who can do no wrong. The believer's actions flow not from any theory of right and wrong but from what an objective observer—a sympathetic non-believer, say—would call an ingested metaphor: the life and personality of Christ. Long and devout study of Christ's life and works has given the believer a model of behavior too subtle and complex for verbal expression but nevertheless trustworthy.

In the same way, fiction provides, at its best, trustworthy but inexpressible models. We ingest metaphors of good, wordlessly learning to behave more like Levin than like Anna (in *Anna Karenina*), more like the transformed Emma (in Jane Austen's novel) than like the Emma we first meet in the book. This subtle, for the most part wordless knowledge is the "truth" great fiction seeks out.

We have said that Helen's surprise at the arrival of the Achaians is to be, in the fiction we are making up, an implied discovery from which springs, for the reader and perhaps for

Helen, some affirmation or recognition of a value. The question we have not quite answered is: How does the writer's working out of plot lead him to Helen's discovery and his own discovery of what he means? Having analyzed what he must dramatically show to make his climax (her surprise and implied recognition) meaningful and convincing, the writer introduces fictional elements each of which carries its burden of meaning. Like any good liar, the writer makes up the most convincing explanations he can think of for why the things that did not really happen might have happened. He toys with various theories of why the Achaians might have behaved as they do—for example, the possibility that, to a man, they are greedy for the treasures of Troy and glad to use any excuse to go after them, or the possibility that they are moved to their action by the extraordinary charisma of Menelaos, or the possibility (absurd but traditional) that they are aroused to action by Helen's beauty. Taken singly, none of these possible explanations will wash, because what they say about reality (what they "mean") does not strike us as true. Our experience of humanity makes it hard for us to believe that *that* many Achaians (or members of any other group) could be so strongly motivated by greed, though some might join in for that reason; we cannot believe in charisma so powerful it could move that many kings, each of whom must have his own concerns and troubles; and as for Helen's beauty, we cannot help feeling that no young woman's beauty can to that degree excel the beauty of all other young women, including some who are sure to say, "Miklos, don't go! Think of the children!" The Achaian code of honor, on the other hand—especially when combined with such lesser motivations as greed (which the legend gives us in Agamemnon at his weaker moments), Menelaos' charisma, and Helen's beauty—offers persuasive cause. By the same process, the writer figures out why the Trojans do what they do and why Helen does not guess what she should have guessed.

Since Helen, in this story, is the central character, her nature

and motivation will be of special importance to the convincingness of the lie. One possible choice, it might seem at first glance,
is to make her an innocent victim. Sheltered and coddled,
brought up among women, married in her girlhood to mighty
Menelaos, she has no real knowledge of her hard-working, hard-
fighting kinsmen, their fanatical loyalty to one another, and
their puritanical code. Though all these qualities might prove
useful to the writer, the decision to make her a victim will be
disastrous. No fiction can have real interest if the central character is not an agent struggling for his or her own goals but a
victim, subject to the will of others. (Failure to recognize that
the central character must act, not simply be acted upon, is the
single most common mistake in the fiction of beginners.) We
care how things turn out because the character cares—our interest comes from empathy—and though we may know more than
the character knows, anticipating dangers the character cannot
see, we understand and to some degree sympathize with the
character's desire, approving what the character approves
(what the character values), even if we sense that the character's ideal is impractical or insufficient. Thus though we can see
at a glance that Captain Ahab is a madman, we affirm his furious hunger to know the truth, so much so that we find ourselves
caught up, like the crew of the *Pequod*, in his lunatic quest. And
thus though we know in our bones that the theory of Raskolnikov is wrong, we share his sense of outrage at the injustice
of things and become accessories in his murder of the cynical
and cruel old pawnbrokeress. If we're bored by the debauched
focal characters of the Marquis de Sade, on the other hand, the
reason is that we find their values and goals repugnant, their
world view too stupid (threatening?) to hold our interest.

Helen, then, must bring her trouble on herself, through the
active pursuit of some goal we believe not wrong-headed. The
nobler the goal, the more interesting the story. We need not
elaborate in detail here the possibilities—her wish, as a child of
Zeus, for more intelligent and sophisticated company, her horror

at the ethnocentricity of the Greeks, her desire for greater dignity and independence, and so on. Whatever the writer's choice for the motivation of Helen, he must think out the implications of her motive, its relationship with the differing community values of the Trojans and the Achaians, and its origins. We may fully realize the implications of her motive only at the moment of recognition, the climax—how (for example) her desire for independence is caught in the crossfire of conflicting community values—but long before that moment we must be shown clearly, not just told, what her driving motive is. To be shown, we must be shown by action; the proof must appear in plot. We must be shown the relationship between Helen's ideal and the functional beliefs of Trojans, on one side, Achaians, on the other, and this too must appear in plot. Some action of Helen's might elicit one reaction from Menelaos, another from Paris, early in the story, and something in the nature of Helen's character, or something in the nature of that early event, should give us clues as to why Helen underestimates Menelaos and the Achaians and perhaps overestimates her potential security with Paris and the Trojans. Finally, if Helen's motive is to be perfectly convincing, we must be shown its origins; and that too means plot. She might remember from her early childhood, for example, some event involving a beloved nurse, once a queen, now a slave—an event that helped to shape Helen's defiant and independent character. All these events, the authenticating proofs for every significant element of the story, the writer must weave into a smoothly flowing, inevitable-seeming plot.

Having done all this, the writer is not quite at the end of his troubles. Every proof the writer thinks up in support of the story's larger elements will have its own implications and exert its own subtle pressure on the story. The old slave he invented in support of Helen's character, if she's to do the work required of her (motivate Helen), must be a vivid and interesting character; otherwise we cannot understand why her influence should be so powerful. But once a vivid and interesting character has been introduced, he or she cannot simply be dropped, forgotten henceforward. Once the character is gone—hanged, let us say—we miss the character; or, to put it another way, we expect the character's return, at least in Helen's memory. It will not be sufficient, the writer will find, simply to mention the old slave's name from time to time. Though her work for the story is done, she must come back, at least briefly, and the question is: What is she to do when she comes back? She can't just stand there. Forced by the necessity of his story to bring her back and provide her with some action, however brief, the writer is forced to think up some further meaning for the character (it may help to ask, in this case, how the slave's defiant independence differs from Helen's). It is partly in this way that the fictional process forces the writer to say more than he thought he could; that is, to make discoveries.

At some point the writer stops planning and starts writing, fleshing out the skeleton that is his plan. Here too he is partly in control of and partly controlled by the fictional process. Again and again, in the process of writing, he will find himself forced to new discoveries. He must create, stroke by stroke, powerfully convincing characters and settings; he must more and more clearly define for himself what his overall theme or idea is; and he must choose and aesthetically justify his genre and style.

Character is created partly by an assembly of facts, including actions, partly by symbolic association. The first needs no comment. Menelaos is, say, rather older than Helen, a famous warrior, a poor rhetorician, a stern king but one easily moved to tears. These are simply facts. The writer makes up or borrows from legend as many of them as he needs, supports them with appropriate habits and gestures, and shows in the behavior of other characters when they deal with Menelaos that the king is who and what he seems. But often our deepest sense of character comes from symbolic association. We frequently learn about fictional characters as we identify people in the game called Smoke, or sometimes called Essences.

In this game the player who is it thinks of some famous personage living or dead, such as Gandhi, Charles de Gaulle, or Frank Sinatra, then tells the other players, "I am a dead Asian," "I am a dead European," "I am a living American," or whatever. The players, in order, try to guess the name of the personage by asking such questions as "What kind of smoke are you?" "What kind of weather are you?" "What kind of animal are you?" "What part of the human anatomy?" And so on. The player who is it answers not in terms of what the personage might have liked to smoke, what weather he might have preferred, etc., but what the personage would *be* if he were incarnated not as a human being but as, say, a certain kind of smoke—cigarette, cigar, pipe, or, more specifically, Virginia Slims, White Owl, or Prince Albert pipe tobacco. As they ask their questions, the players develop a powerful sense of the personality they're seeking, and when finally, on the basis of the information they've been given, someone makes the right guess, the result is likely to be an orgasmic sense of relief. Obviously the game cannot be played with the intellect; it depends on metaphoric intuition. Yet anyone who plays the game with good players will discover that the metaphors that describe the personage whose name is being sought have, at least cumulatively, a remarkable precision.

In fiction, characterization by symbolic association can be infinitely more precise than it can ever be in the game, partly because (in the final draft) the metaphors are carefully considered, and partly because we are dealing with a consistently good player. The writer may use metaphor directly, as when he tells us Paris is like a dapper, slightly foolish fox, or he may work for symbolic association in subtler ways. He may place a character in the weather that metaphorically expresses his nature, so that unwittingly we make a connection between the gloom of Menelaos and the gloom of the weather at his back. Or the writer may subtly incline us to identify Helen's character with the elegantly wrought knife with which she carves.

In fleshing out his characters, the writer does not ordinarily think out every implication of every image he introduces at the time he introduces it. He writes by feel, intuitively, imagining the scene vividly and copying down its most significant details, keeping the fictional dream alive, sometimes writing in a thoughtless white heat of "inspiration," drawing on his unconscious, trusting his instincts, hoping that when he looks back at it later, in cool objectivity, the scene will work. So he proceeds through the story, event by event, character by character. Each time he sits down for another day's work, he may read over what he's done, making minor revisions and getting a run on the passage where he stopped. Different writers have different ways of working, but the likelihood is that the writer's chief concern, at this stage, is with achieving a totally convincing, efficient, and elegant action. With some exceptions, the details he brings in he brings in for that purpose, none deeper.

But at some point, perhaps when he's finished his first draft, the writer begins to work in another way. He begins to brood over what he's written, reading it over and over, patiently, endlessly, letting his mind wander, sometimes to Picasso or the Great Pyramid, sometimes to the possible philosophical implications of Menelaos' limp (a detail he introduced by impulse, because it seemed right). Reading in this strange way lines he has known by heart for weeks, he discovers odd tics his unconscious has sent up to him, perhaps curious accidental repetitions of imagery: The brooch Helen threw at Menelaos the writer has described, he discovers, with the same phrase he used in describing, much later, the seal on the message for help sent to the Trojans' allies. Why? he wonders. Just as dreams have meaning, whether or not we can penetrate the meaning, the writer assumes that the accidents in his writing may have significance. He tries various possibilities; for instance, the possibility that Helen's wish for independence is partly self-delusion. The idea grows on him. He reads through the story again and becomes increasingly convinced. He makes tiny alterations. Helen's character deepens and flowers. In response, Menelaos slightly changes; so does Paris. Slowly, painstakingly, with the patience that separates a Beethoven from men of equal genius but less divine stubbornness, the great writer builds the large, rockfirm thought that is his fiction.

What happens in the writer's development of characters happens also in his development of atmosphere and setting. The megaliths and walls that form the salient feature of the cities of the Achaians, antithetical to the flowered walkways and the topless towers of Ilium, grow more stern, more alarming in their solidity with each revision. Menelaos' scepter, which he uses as a cane, takes on daemonic force.

Since somewhere near the end of his planning of the fiction, the writer has known pretty clearly what the general idea or theme of the work is to be. By *theme* here we mean not "message"—a word no good writer likes applied to his work—but the general subject, as the theme of an evening of debates may be World-Wide Inflation. Since early on, it has been clear that in our Helen story the theme has had to do with community and individual values. (Another writer, making different choices about plot and character, might well have emerged with a different theme, such as Life versus Art—the Achaians on one side, the Trojans on the other, with Helen in the crossfire as both wife and lover, both keeper of the household goods and fanatical artist when she works at her loom—or the writer might have organized the story in terms of Body and Soul.) Given his choice of community and individual values as his theme, the writer sharpens and clarifies his ideas, or finds out exactly what it is that he must say, testing his beliefs against reality as the story represents it, by examining every element in the story for its possible implications with regard to his theme. He thinks about Menelaos' scepter, for example. It occurs to him that the scepter might be a legacy from Menelaos' father, hence a symbol of, among other things, tradition or continuity (the detail might not come up if the theme were Life and Art); and once this has occurred to him he may be led to wonder if tradition is viewed in the same way or in different ways by the Achaians and the Trojans, and, if the latter, whether Paris might also be given some appropriate symbol, and if so, what? And precisely what does this symbol imply? The thought of tradition brought down from fathers to sons—a thought reinforced by the inevitable prominence of old King Priam, Paris's father, in the story's later segments—may lead him to muse on Helen's lineage, half human, half divine. Granted that the writer would have difficulty believing in the literal rape of Helen's mother by Zeus, what might the symbolic double heritage mean? What legitimacy can be found for the metaphor?

Finally, the writer must find for his story what seem to him the most appropriate genre and style. Here too his choices have implications. In origin, the story of Helen is of course epic—a dead form. What happens if, throwing caution to the winds, the writer decides to revive it? As practiced by Homer, the epic was a queer sort of serious yarn: The poet tells, often, of impossible things and makes no bones about the fact of their impossibility; yet he does not, like the yarn-spinner, wink at us, encouraging us to enjoy the lie for the cunning and wit of the liar. Neither does he, like a tale narrator, make a point of distancing his story in time and space, or of persuading us by tone and atmosphere that we should suspend disbelief. When human beings are involved (Achilles' talking horses warning him of his death), the poet speaks seriously. We must read the event as expressionistic truth, as when Gregor Samsa woke up and discovered himself changed to a cockroach. When the gods are involved, the poet may speak in a way more troublesome to our modern mind-set. For Homer and his audience, the gods are simply, somehow, outside forces that can daemonically enter or otherwise act on human beings, influencing their lives. (Some of Homer's gods have traditional names like Zeus; others have names like Confusion.) Since the way in which the gods work can never be known, Homer makes up humanlike behavior for them, sometimes apologizes by comedy for the artifice, yet means what he says. When divine wisdom gives way to some other force, it is *as if* Hera has put Zeus to sleep by a sexual seduction. The event is comic, the effect partly tragic; and to make things more confusing, these same divine artifices can feel sorrow we respect, not at all the comic wailing of clowns. Though on reflection we may understand Homer's method and reconstruct the ancient mindset, I think we must say that we simply cannot think like that. To revive the epic, the modern writer must commit himself to irony and a detached, self-conscious objectivity foreign to the original epic style. He cannot write an epic but only an earnest parody that works chiefly as a study of the artistic mind or as a comment on art by art. Perhaps this parodic revival of the genre might work for the writer who has chosen to treat the Helen story as a fictional exploration of Life versus Art, but if the writer's theme is private and community values, the revival of epic form seems fruitless.

What happens if he chooses to tell the story as a tale? The inherent dignity and solemnity of the form would obviously be suitable to the content of the story, and at first glance the materials seem easily adaptable to the tale's basic rules. The setting of a tale is customarily remote in either time or space or both and is presented with a mixture of vagueness and generality on one hand and with meticulously exact detail on the other. The writer's care in supplying exact detail encourages credence; and the remoteness, together with the vagueness and generality, tends to prevent the reader from considering the reality or unreality of the setting. The landscape of a tale is of a kind likely to inspire the reader's wonder—lonely moors, sunny meadows, wild mountains, dark forests, desolate seacoasts—and both natural and man-made features of the setting are frequently of great age, suggesting a past charged with traditions and values that impose themselves on the will of the characters.

Tale characters are designed to be convincing without suggesting comparison with real people. They behave in recognizably human ways, but they may be supernatural beings; and even when they seem to be in most respects like ordinary men and women, they tend to be a little larger than life and may possess extraordinary powers. Like the settings in the tale, the characters usually have a certain remoteness. They may be counts, kings, knights, rich merchants, peasants, cobblers. Often they are entirely evil or entirely good (the superlative is common in the tale—"the richest," "the fairest," "the oldest," "the wisest"). Although characters may be complex, the details of their complexity are often blurred, as if by time. Only the significant aspects are retained in the narrator's memory, and often the narrator, it is clear, has the story at second hand, perhaps by ancient oral tradition. The characters' actions—the plot of the tale—may or may not obey the laws of cause and effect operative in the actual world, but even when they do not, they seem natural because of their psychological or poetic truth. The reality of the world of the tale, in other words, is that of a moral universe. What ought to happen, possible or not, does happen.

For the Helen story we've been working out, much in the genre of the tale seems promising. The supernatural elements in the Helen tradition fit naturally with tale presentation, though the essential gothicism of the genre might incline us to treat Greek gods and goddesses as rather like witches; the traditional effect of the story's main characters, all larger than life, is appropriate for the genre; and the tale's customary emphasis on oldness and tradition might naturally spring interesting ideas and developments not guessed in advance by the writer. Yet we notice certain problems that may in the end prove insurmountable. The principle of causality in a tale is psychological and morally expressionistic, or poetic: It should not be the Achaians who come to fill Helen with surprise—forces outside her—but a necessary doom arising from her own psychology, some suppressed truth that at last rises to take revenge. If we say that Helen left her people from vanity, as the "fairest of all the Achaians," then the claims of a tale version of the Helen story might be something like this: She is told that a thousand

Achaian ships have been sighted, and when she flies out, ter-
rified, to look, she sees that they are all filled with armed women
who look exactly like herself. The possibilities in this are perhaps interesting and might encourage the writer to work back
from the climax to fill in the logical necessities of this different
conclusion; but here we encounter the second large problem in
presenting the story of Helen as a tale.

Though it's partly a matter of the individual writer's intuition and taste, it may seem that the new ending clashes too
noticeably with the Greek story as we know it. Indeed, the
whole tone of the tale genre clashes rather fiercely with our
feelings about Greece and Troy. Though the war between the
two took place long ago and in a far-away country, it does not
feel to us remote in time and space. One might conceivably
write a tale in which Queen Elizabeth and King Henry (any
King Henry) have parts as minor characters; one might possibly
write a tale about Napoleon and Josephine; or one might write a
tale including Charlemagne—as Calvino does in *The Nonexistent Knight* (not a pure tale but a generic hybrid). But Greek
tradition seems somehow too full of sunlight and sharp imagery,
too charged with Homeric immediacy, to accommodate the
mood of a tale. The only possible solution, perhaps, would be to
change the locale and all the characters' names, placing the
arrival of the mysterious ships off the coast of, say, ancient
Norway.

How the story would work set as a yarn we need not elaborate. We see at once that a yarn-spinner would have to be
introduced; and some implied reason for his spinning of the
yarn; and justification would have to be found for telling so
serious a story comically. Such adaptations are not impossible,
though the project may seem unpromising. The yarn-spinner
might be, for once, an old woman, and her purpose in telling the
story might be subtly feminist. Making Helen her heroine, a
shrewd woman who at every turn comically outwits her male
"superiors," she escapes to freedom. Here, if not sooner, the yarn

might go dark, becoming a generic hybrid (yarn crossed with realistic story): Helen's ultimate failure, tonally conflicting with all that went before, might give, however subtly, an angry, revolutionary tone to the conclusion. The reader's indignation at the unhappy ending might be made to release the meaning—or, in this case, implied message—that women, however they may struggle and whatever their brilliance, are always beaten in the end by male chauvinism, a condition that ought not to prevail. If all this were done in too obvious a fashion, the story would of course be boring; but for the writer with sufficient lightness of touch and a gift for authentic humor, the yarn hybrid might have a good deal of subtlety and interest, every detail serving its feminist theme, the relative power of men and women.

Finally, the story might be told more or less realistically, as Gide treats Greek legend in his novella "Theseus." The story's supernatural elements, if not suppressed entirely, would in this case be carefully played down, treated as givens and quickly left behind for the story's main action, already realistic in nature. Since the plot we've worked out is inherently one suitable for realistic presentation, we need say no more.

The last major element that may modify the fictional thought is style. In true yarn and tale presentation, style is a given. If the story is presented in the form of a realistic novel, novella, or short story, or in some hybrid cross of realism and something else, the writer's choice of style becomes a serious consideration. We need not spell out all the various possibilities of stylistic choice (to do so would be impossible in any case); it will be enough simply to suggest that each choice has implications. The writer must decide what point of view he will use, what diction level, what "voice," what psychic-distance range. If he has Helen tell the story in the first person, he has the problem, at once, of establishing the information Helen herself misses (the nature of the Achaians and the Trojans). In any long fiction, Henry James remarked, use of the first-person point of view is barbaric. James may go too far, but his point is worth considering. First person locks us in one character's mind, locks us to one kind of diction throughout, locks out possibilities of going deeply into various characters' minds, and so forth. What is sometimes called the "third-person-limited point of view," or "third person subjective," has some of the same drawbacks for a long piece of fiction. (This point of view is essentially the same as first person except that each "I" is changed to "she" or "Helen.") The traditional third-person-omniscient point of view, in which the story is told by an unnamed narrator (a persona of the author) who can dip into the mind and thoughts of any character, though he focuses primarily on no more than two or three, gives the writer greatest range and freedom. When he pleases, this narrator can speak in his own voice, filling in necessary background or offering objective observations; yet when the scene is intense and his presence would be intrusive, he can write in the third-person-limited point of view, vanishing for the moment from our consciousness. A related point of view is that of the essayist-narrator, much like the traditional omniscient narrator except that he (or she) has a definite voice and definite opinions, which may or may not be reliable. This narrator may be virtually a character in the story, having a name and some distant relationship to the people and events he describes, or may be simply a particularized but unnamed voice. The choice of point of view will largely determine all other choices with regard to style—vulgar, colloquial, or formal diction, the length and characteristic speed of sentences, and so on. What the writer must consider, obviously, is the extent to which point of view, and all that follows from it, comments on the characters, actions, and ideas. Vulgar diction in the telling of the Helen story would clearly create a white-hot irony, probably all but unmanageable. Colloquial diction and relatively short sentences would have the instant effect of humanizing once elevated characters and events. Highly formal diction and all that goes along with the traditional omniscient narrator might seem immediately appropriate for the seriousness of the story, but it can easily backfire, providing not suitable pomp but mere pompousness. And some choices in point of view, as well as in other stylistic elements, may have more direct bearing on the theme than would others. For instance, the "town" point of view, in which the voice in the story is some unnamed spokesman for all the community—among the most famous examples is Faulkner's "A Rose for Emily"—might have the immediate effect of foregrounding the story's controlling idea, conflicting community values versus personal values.

We have looked enough at the fictional process to see how the conventional writer's choices, from such large choices as subject, plot, character, setting, and theme to choices about the smallest detail of style, can all help him discover what it is he wants to say. We have seen that the process is at every stage both intuitive and intellectual: The writer chooses his subject because it appeals to him—a matter of feeling—but in developing it, first in his plan, then in his writing, he continually depends both on intellectual faculties, such as critical abstraction and musing speculation, and on intuition—his general sense of how the world works, his impulses and feelings. Having come this far, we can get better perspective on our original questions about aesthetic interest and truth in conventional fiction.

Both for the writer and for the careful reader after him, everything that happens in a well-constructed story, from major events to the most trifling turn of phrase, is a matter of aesthetic interest. Since the writer has chosen every element with care, and has revised and repeatedly re-revised in an attempt to reach something like aesthetic perfection, every element we encounter is worth savoring. Every character is sufficiently vivid and interesting for his function; every scene is just long enough, just rich enough; every metaphor is polished; no symbol stands out crudely from its matrix of events, yet no resonance goes completely unheard, too slyly muffled by the literal. Though we read the work again and again and again, we can never seem to get to the bottom of it.

Naturally such subtlety—a story containing such a treasury of pleasures—is achieved at some cost. To work so beautifully, it cannot work as quickly or simply as does a comic book. (The greater the subtlety, the greater the sacrifice.) It is for this reason that the reader who loves great fiction is willing to put up with an opening as slow as that of Mann's "Death in Venice," an opening that might seem tedious to those who read nothing but *Howard the Duck*. This clearly does not mean that the serious writer should make a point of being tiresome and intellectual to drive away dolts. If he respects the reader, if he honestly considers what he himself would like to read, the writer will choose the most immediately and powerfully interesting characters and events he can think of. He will go for, as they say, dramaturgy. No two writers, as we've recognized, will think of quite the same characters and events when they look for what appeals to them. Some writers enjoy stories of the end of the world; some prefer fascinating tea parties. But if the writer writes only of what honestly interests him, and if he thinks of his work not simply as thoughtful exploration, as it should be, but also as entertainment, he cannot fail to have, at least for some group of serious, devoted readers, both immediate and lasting interest.

If the writer's work is fully successful, we are likely to say of it, without thinking too carefully what it is that we mean, that the work is "true." We are in a position to see now that our judgment, however unconsidered, may well be accurate. We have seen that even such a relatively trivial decision as the choice of diction level can alter the story's implications in striking ways. Those who claim that fiction has no relationship to truth make much of this. They point out that if we use short sentences, short vowels, and hard consonants, we get a totally different effect, on any subject, than we do if we use long sentences, long vowels, and nasal or liquid consonants. No one would deny that this is true. But what needs to be noticed is that the good writer makes each choice he makes because it seems to him appropriate. A fictional element can be appropriate or not by only one of two standards: It is appropriate to the work as an art object without reference to reality, or it is appropriate as we test it against our sense of the actual. It seems doubtful that art's elements can ever be appropriate only to one another. The colors in a painting without recognizable images may be said to be appropriate only to one another, but it is human emotion that judges, testing against itself. As for fiction, in any case, it seems fair to argue that, since no narrative beyond a certain length can hold interest without some such profluence as a causal relation of events (by either real-world logic, comic mock-logic, or poetic logic), no narrative except a very short one can escape real-world relevance: Our comparison of the work and reality is automatic and instantaneous. To say that a style feels appropriate to a subject is to say, then, that we believe it in some way helps us to see the subject truly.

Fiction seeks out truth. Granted, it seeks a poetic kind of truth, universals not easily translatable into moral codes. But part of our interest as we read is in learning how the world works; how the conflicts we share with the writer and all other human beings can be resolved, if at all; what values we can affirm and, in general, what the moral risks are. The writer who can't distinguish truth from a peanut-butter sandwich can never write good fiction. What he affirms we deny, throwing away his book in indignation; or if he affirms nothing, not even our oneness in sad or comic helplessness, and insists that he's perfectly right to do so, we confute him by closing his book. Some bad men write good books, admittedly, but the reason is that when they're writing they're better men than when they beat their wives and children. When he writes, the man of impetuous bad character has time to reconsider. The fictional process helps him say what he might not have said that same night in the tavern.

Good men, on the other hand, need not necessarily write good books. Good-heartedness and sincerity are no substitute for rigorous pursuit of the fictional process.

None of this high-minded rhetoric is meant to deny the fact that fiction is a kind of play. The writer works out what he thinks as much for the joy of it as for any other reason. Yet the play has its uses and earnestness. It is sometimes remarked, not by enemies of fiction but by people who love it, that whereas scientists and politicians work for progress, the writer of fiction restates what has always been known, finding new expression for familiar truths, adapting to the age truths that may seem outmoded. It is true that, in treating human emotion, with which we're all familiar, the writer discovers nothing, merely clarifies for the moment, and that in treating what Faulkner called "the eternal verities," the writer treats nothing unheard of, since people have been naming and struggling to organize their lives around eternal verities for thousands of years. It may even be true that many good writers feel indifferent to their work once they've finished it. When they've checked through the galley proofs, they may never look again at the labor they've devoted so much time to. But the fact remains that art produces the most important progress civilization knows. Restating old truths and adapting them to the age, applying them in ways they were never before applied, stirring up emotion by the inherent power of narrative, visual image, or music, artists crack the door to the morally necessary future. The age-old idea of human dignity comes to apply even to the indigent, even to slaves, even to immigrants, now recently even to women. This is not to say that great writing is propaganda. But because the fictional process selects those fit for it, and because a requirement of that process is strong empathetic emotion, it turns out that the true writer's fundamental concern—his reason for finding a subject interesting in the first place—is likely to be humane. He sees injustice or misunderstanding in the world around him, and he cannot keep it out of his story. It may be true that he writes principally for the love of writing, and that in the heat of creation he cares as much about the convincing description of Helen's face as he does about the verities her story brings to focus, but the true literary artist is a far cry from those who create "toy fiction," good or bad—TV entertainments to take the pensioner's mind off his dismal existence, self-regarding aesthetic jokes, posh super-realism, where emotion is ruled out and idea is thought vulgar, or nostalgia fiction, or pornography. The true writer's joy in the fictional process is his pleasure in discovering, by means he can trust, what he believes and can affirm for all time. When the last trump plays, he will be listening, criticizing, figuring out the proper psychic distance. It should be added, for honesty's sake, that the true literary artist and the man or woman who makes "toy fiction" may be the same person in different moods. Even on the subject of high seriousness, we must beware of reckless high seriousness.

4

Metafiction, Deconstruction, and Jazzing Around

Not all fiction, old or new, works by the principles we've been examining so far; in fact, though the theory we've been tracing out has been the dominant theory of fiction since the seventeenth century or so, most of the literature of humanity works by other sets of principles. The *Iliad* has no "characters," at least not in the modern sense—rounded, complex human beings. *The Divine Comedy* and *Beowulf* have, at least in the Aristotelian sense, no "plot"—no causally related sequence of events. And many great works, from the *Gilgamesh* to *Paradise Lost*—if not Pound's *Cantos*—proceed not by rendered actions, as Henry James would have events proceed, but by set speeches.

Changes in narrative method reflect changes in the way human beings see—or think they ought to see—the world. In a strongly authoritarian age, an age in which kings and counsellors are revered as innately better than ordinary men and women, people tend to see fiction as a vehicle of instruction. By means of fiction, things the authorities know to be true are sugar-coated and passed down to those for whom the truth is not so visible. It is hard to speak fairly of authoritarian ages, both because they're naturally repugnant to the democratic spirit and because they are forever watching from the wings, hoping to seize the stage again. But some of the greatest literature in the world comes out of such ages, and we need to understand how that literature works to understand how our own works and why our own, too, is fated to suffer constant change.

Authoritarian literature tends to work by the allegorical method, or at least gets its profluence from abstract logic (the development of an argument from *a* to *b* to *c*), not by *energeia*. Take the greatest work of this type in English (or, rather, ancient English), *Beowulf*. The narrative is presented in three large sections. In the first, a monster called Grendel persecutes the Danish people until a heroic friend from another tribe, Beowulf, kills the monster; in the second section, the monster's mother attacks the Danes, hoping to avenge her monstrous son's death, and Beowulf kills her too; and in the third section, Beowulf, now an old, old man and king of the Geatish nation, fights a dragon and dies himself in the act of killing it. The second section—Beowulf and Grendel's mother—proceeds causally from the first, but only by accident; and the third section—Beowulf and the dragon—has no causal roots in the first or second sections. It is not because Beowulf killed Grendel and his dam that he must now kill the dragon. Many years have passed, and so far as we can tell the dragon never met Grendel or his mother.

The principle of profluence in *Beowulf* is abstract, not dramatic. Grendel is identified in the poem as a symbol of unreason, one who wars against all order and loves chaos. Grendel, in other words, represents a total malfunction of one of the three parts of the Platonic tripartite soul (cf. Plato's *Republic*), the *intellectual*. Grendel's dam represents a total malfunction of the second part of the tripartite soul, the *irascible* (the part that, like a good watchdog or soldier, should fight for right against wrong). And the dragon represents a total malfunction of the third part, the *concupiscent* (that is, the part that deals with things physical, such as food, wealth, comfort). The coming of Grendel's dam in the second section of the poem seems causally related to the death of Grendel, but in fact this is not the principle of selection the poet was using; otherwise he could have found some causal way of bringing in the dragon. Causality was simply not what interested him; he was shaping a poem that would illustrate, or demonstrate, the relationship between the soul's three parts, showing them at their best in Beowulf and at their worst in the monsters. Readers familiar with the poem will realize that the poet was doing much more besides; but the whole ingenious structure works by the principle I've been pointing out, not dramatization (in Aristotle's sense) but allegorical expression, or demonstration. The poet who truly dramatizes a conflict, carefully exploring causal-event chains, cannot be sure what the end of his story will be until he gets there. For him, fiction is a means of discovery. For the allegorist, on the other hand, fiction is largely, though perhaps not exclusively, a means of expressing what the writer already knows.

A literary work need not be allegorical to be a demonstration rather than an exploration. Any narrative that moves from scene to scene and episode to episode not according to the exigencies of cause and effect but according to some abstract scheme is likely to be a demonstration. The picaresque novel, which conventionally follows some hero from one social setting to another and another, demonstrating the folly of each social context, is essentially as abstract and instructional as *Pilgrim's Progress*. Or a novel in the shape of a fictional biography may proceed according to the requirements of some abstract design. In *David Copperfield*, for instance, episodes seem to progress randomly, like real life, until one notices the controlling concern with love and marriage. Dickens chooses events, in other words, for their relevance to an abstract central question. At Dickens' point in the development of the novel, it is hard to tell whether we are dealing mainly with exploration or mainly with demonstration. (Obviously both are involved.) In some Dickens novels, such as *A Tale of Two Cities*, we sense pretty strongly the preacherly method, demonstration as opposed to exploration; in others, especially late novels like *Great Expectations*, we may feel the two impulses warring in the writer's mind.

Cataloguing narratives as one thing or another would serve no useful purpose at the moment. What counts here is the general observation that fiction has for centuries existed on a continuum running between authoritarian and existential. Certain books, like the *Iliad*, served their original audience as, in effect, trustworthy history, lawbook, even bible; others, like Apollonios Rhodios' *Argonautica*, show only comic or ironic respect for the traditions and accepted patterns of their culture and seem to offer no answers, only difficult questions. One kind of narrative, the kind I describe as authoritarian, is sometimes said to look at its story line "spatially," each of its elements existing for the sake of a predetermined "end" or conclusion. This is almost inevitably the kind of fiction produced by a writer who composes his narrative by working backward from the climax, and in practice any well-made story may be suspected of having been built this way, since in the final draft, we can be sure, the writer will have introduced whatever preparation his ending needs—however existentially he may in fact have arrived at his ending. For some contemporary readers and critics, a narrative that seems to them spatially conceived is morally distressing. This may be no more than a personal quirk of those readers and critics affected; but the quirk does have some root in reality: Metaphysics and unjustified notions of human certainty had more than a little to do with the holocaust and American fire-bombings, not to mention atomic bombings, napalm, and the rest. It is perhaps largely for this reason that we have seen since World War II, all over the world, a rise of non-profluent fiction (actions leading nowhere, as in the plays of Samuel Beckett) and unended fiction (as in John Fowles' *The French Lieutenant's Woman*).

Critics who have focused their attention on unconventional recent fiction have used a variety of terms to identify it, most of them apparently interchangeable—"fabulation," "post-modernism," "metafiction," "deconstructive fiction," and so forth. To get a clear sense of the kinds of interest and truth available in unconventional fiction as it is presently practiced, it will be useful to begin by clearing up the critical language. For our present discussion, let us scrap the terms "post-modernism" and "fabulation," since "post-modernism" sets up only a vague antithesis to "modernism," meaning only, in effect, more like Italo Calvino than like Saul Bellow, and since "fabulation" seems to mean nothing but "unconventional." "Metafiction," as critics generally use the word, is a more precise term. It means fiction that, both in style and theme, investigates fiction. As we have seen, conventional fiction can be an instrument for examining the world; and, like any humanly devised instrument, it can malfunction. Like a faulty microscope or telescope, it can persuade us of things that are not true. For example, the conventional love-story ending as we find it in Jane Austen can subtly persuade the careless reader (though Jane Austen never intended it) that for every woman there is some one perfect man. Needless to say, the more powerful a literary convention becomes—the more frequently people write books in careful or shabby imitation of Jane Austen's—the more perverse the convention's impact. Human beings can hardly move without models for their behavior, and from the beginning of time, in all probability, we have known no greater purveyor of models than story-telling. Put it this way: Say that, at a certain time in a certain country, some writer —perhaps imitating someone he admires—creates a hero whose life motto is "Never complain, never explain." The motto has a certain ring to it; it's the kind of thing one might consider putting up on the wall in the bathroom of one's children. In one lifelike situation after another, we see this hero bearing up under adversity, scorned for things he is not guilty of, laughed at for things he would be praised for if the whole truth were known. Again and again (in this same, thrilling book), we see our hero giving orders he secretly wishes he didn't need to give, making painful decisions that, for certain lofty reasons, he cannot explain to his friends and loved ones. The effect on the reader of this lonely, lofty hero could be very great indeed—but not necessarily healthy. If such heroes occur in very many plays and novels, if the appeal of such a character becomes widespread, then democracy, even common decency, is undermined. We have been taught to admire, submit to, or behave like the well-meaning Nazi officer, the business-world tyrant, or the moral fanatic. Nothing in the world has greater power to enslave than does fiction.

One way of undermining fiction's harmful effects is the writing of metafiction: a story that calls attention to its methods and shows the reader what is happening to him as he reads. In this kind of fiction, needless to say, the law of the "vivid and continuous dream" is no longer operative; on the contrary, the breaks in the dream are as important as the dream. This general method is far from new, though for reasons I've suggested it is especially popular at the moment. In the *Argonautica*, Apollonios repeatedly jerks the reader awake with some seemingly perverse misuse of epic tradition, or with some unexpected, slightly frigid joke, or some seemingly needless, ponderous comment. But when we've finished the poem, we can never again look with the same innocent admiration at the machismo of Homer's epics, or praise the warrior's shame culture above the civilized man's guilt culture. We find a gentler use of metafictional techniques in Sterne's *Tristram Shandy* or Fielding's *Tom Jones*. In recent fiction, works that call insistent attention to their artifice are everywhere—Ionesco, Beckett, Barth, Barthelme, Borges, Fowles, Calvino, Gass, and so on.

It is useful to distinguish between metafiction and fictional deconstruction, though technically the latter term encloses the former. All metafictions are deconstructions; not all deconstructions are metafictions.

No common contemporary critical term raises hackles more quickly than the term "deconstruction," and rightly so, since those who use the term almost always sound wildly confused.

Probably the truth is that they are not so much confused as hamstrung by worship of Heidegger. At any rate, behind the deconstructionists' dazzling cloud of language lie certain more or less indisputable facts: that language carries values with it, sometimes values we do not recognize as we speak and would not subscribe to if we noticed their presence in what we say; and that art (music, painting, literature, etc.) is language. That language carries values is obvious. Again and again this book speaks of the writer as "he," though many of the best writers I have read or have taught in writing classes are female. English, like most languages, is covertly male chauvinist. It is also, as the novelist Harold Brodkey points out, covertly Christian. Nearly all our most resonant words and images carry a trace of Neoplatonic Christianity. Even so innocent a word as "friend" has overtones. In feudal times it meant one's lord and protector; in Anglo-Saxon times it meant the opposite of "fiend." We can of course read a book about friends without ever consciously invoking the undercurrents of the word; but where the friendship grows intense, in this story we're reading, we are almost sure to encounter images of light or warmth, flower or garden imagery, hunger, sacrifice, blood, and so on. The very form of the story, its orderly beginning, middle, and end, is likely to hint at a Christian metaphysic.

Deconstruction is the practice of taking language apart, or taking works of art apart, to discover their unacknowledged inner workings. Whatever value this approach may or may not have as literary criticism, it is one of the main methods of contemporary (and sometimes ancient) fiction. Deconstructive fiction is parallel to revisionist history in that it tells the story from the other side or from some queer angle that casts doubt on the generally accepted values handed down by legend. Whereas metafiction deconstructs by directly calling attention to fiction's tricks, deconstructive fiction retells the story in such a way that the old version loses credit. Shakespeare's *Hamlet* can be seen as a work of this kind. In the revenge tragedies Shakespeare's audience was familiar with, some ghost or friend or other plot-device lays on the hero the burden of avenging some crime. The genre is by nature righteous and self-confident, authoritarian: There is no doubt that vengeance is the hero's duty, and our pleasure as we watch is in seeing justice done, however painful the experience. Shakespeare's *Hamlet* deconstructs all this. Despite Horatio's certainty, we become increasingly doubtful of the ghost's authority as the play progresses, so that we become more and more concerned with Hamlet's tests of people and of himself; and even if we choose to believe that the ghost's story was true, we become increasingly unclear about whether Hamlet would be right to kill the king who usurped his father's throne—at any rate, Claudius becomes less and less the stock villain, and Hamlet, as he proceeds through the play, becomes more and more guilty himself.

Except for the earliest literature we know about—the Akkadian *Gilgamesh*, certain parts of the Bible, and the epics of Homer—all great literature has, to some extent, a deconstructive impulse. This is of course only natural: If the business of the first man is to create, the business of the second is at least partly to correct. Throughout the history of Western civilization, we encounter a few great moments of creation—moments when the deconstructive impulse seems relatively slight—and a great many stretches of time that seem mainly devoted to taking the machinery apart and putting it together again in some new wrong way. Though the Beowulf-poet was deconstructing old pagan legends of heroic derring-do, his main impulse seems to have been *con*structive: the creation of a myth that would fuse all that was best in the old pagan and the new Christian vision. Dante, too, was mainly constructive, fusing the classical and the modern by means of a new truth-principle, what might be described (not quite fairly) as a form of emotivism: "Truth is that which one can say without shame before Beatrice." And one might mention other such moments, most recently the advent of James Joyce.

The interest in metafiction and the interest in deconstructive fiction (when the last is not cast in metafictional form) differ in obvious ways. The appeal of metafiction may be almost entirely intellectual. If we laugh, we do not do so heartily, as when we laugh at or with an interesting lifelike character; we laugh thinly, with a feeling of slight superiority, as we laugh at wise-cracks or "wit." If we grieve, we grieve like philosophers, not like people who have lost loved ones. Mainly, we think. We think about the writer's allusions, his use of unexpected devices, his effrontery in breaking the rules. Other forms of decon-struction—other than metafictional, that is—can achieve greater emotional power. For example, retelling the Beowulf story from the point of view of the monster Grendel, one gets not only whatever emotional effect can be wrung out of Grendel's trag-edy, but also whatever grief the experienced reader may feel in seeing the grand old forms of Western civilization revealed as rather shoddy, certainly manipulative and tyrannical, and prob-ably poetic lies in the first place.

None of this is meant to suggest that deconstructive fiction is better than metafiction, or vice versa, or that either of these is better or worse than conventional fiction. That each has its val-ues is evident from the fact that each has its earnest adherents, some of them ready to kill at the faintest hint that what they love is not loved universally.

What we enjoy we enjoy; dispute is useless. And one of the things human beings most enjoy is discovery. We may go along for years without ever noticing that the third-person-limited point of view is essentially sappy. And then one day in metafic-tion one sees that point of view mocked, all its foolishness laid bare, and one laughs with delight. The metafictionist shows us, for instance, that the third-person-limited point of view forces the writer into phony suspense. Say a story begins with this event: A man named Alex Strugatsky is taking his Saturday morning ballet class when his mistress, the wife of the local Chief of Police, comes in to stand watching. Alex is distressed—

he does not want their affair known, lest the police chief shoot him; but also he does not want to be impolite, because his mistress, Genevieve Rochelle, is a beauty. If we start off this story in the sensible omniscient point of view, as Chekhov would, we can get the important facts in right away and get on to what's really interesting, such as: What will Alex do? Do his fellow dancers notice? And so on. In the omniscient point of view one might write:

> One Saturday morning when Alex Strugatsky was taking his dancing class, he happened to look over, while balancing on his toes, and see his mistress, Genevieve Rochelle, wife of the local Chief of Police, standing in the doorway. Good grief, thought Strugatsky, blushing, looking around in horror at the faces of his fellow dancers—mostly middle-aged women who had come there to work off fat.

Notice what happens when the writer limits himself to the thoughts of the central character, mentioning nothing not directly present in the character's mind.

> It was a Saturday morning like any other, the middle-aged fat women of his dancing class laboring around him, the piano punching out uh-*one*, uh-*two*, the teacher floating through the motions, sour-pussed, when suddenly, unsteadily balancing on his toes, Alex Strugatsky looked over at the brightly lit doorway and saw—her! He swung his head around, studying each fat little face in turn, but so far no one had noticed. Would they recognize her if they saw her there? Probably they would. He imagined himself crying out, "No, please! please!" and being shot in the head.

Needless to say, there is a place—in comedy—for such silly hysteria. But it's odd to think how serious all those writers of the thirties and forties were who used this point of view—the same people who, in movies, used solemn voice-over. Or again, the metafictionist may show us, by cunningly misusing this point of view, how third person limited makes narcissists of us all. Alex has gotten away from his dance class and is sitting with Genevieve in her car:

> He did not mind, he thought, her slow way of draw-
> ing the cigarette from its pack or even her long hesitation
> before she reached gropingly for the matches on the dash,
> but the arched eyebrow that accompanied it all, and the
> way she never even glanced through the windshield to see
> if anyone was watching—those were inexcusable! He felt
> himself shaping a frown and caught himself, then covered
> his mouth with one hand, lest the frown sneak back.

All this analyzing of every little gesture on Genevieve's part and Alex's own would be, in real life, the mark of a man deeply paranoid. In our fiction it occurs because the writer has no other way of saying what happens except by somehow putting it into Alex's head.

It might be argued that a clever writer of metafictions could make fun, if he wishes, of any of the standard points of view. That is true and not true. It is probably the case that any human activity can legitimately be made fun of, and that a clever metafictionist could make us laugh at the noblest devices of Dostoevsky or Mann. But the smart writer of metafictions is se-lective about what he pokes fun at, and part of our interest as we read his work comes from our recognition that the folly he points out is significant; that is, it is not only silly, once we look at it closely, but it is in some sense perverse: It pushes wrong values.

Theoretically all non-conventional fiction can be described as either metafiction or deconstructive fiction or both, but secretly—intuitively—we know that much of what we read, or see on stage or on the screen, is neither. It has no theory, it makes no grand claims. It's just jazzing around.

One of the best things narrative can do is jazz around. The Marx Brothers, W. C. Fields, Buster Keaton, old-time Saturday morning cartoons (not the new, cheap ones), certain great fake-profound movies like *The Magician* and *La Strada*. There can be no point in making up an aesthetic theory for jazzing around, but if some fool were to do it, he would find it hard to avoid at least the following basic principles. When a writer is jazzing around, he may not feel a powerful need to create consistent, profound, well-rounded characters. In fact, he might start with an elderly Jew crying on a bus and transform him without notice to a boy of eleven, then to a sparrow, then to the Queen of Poland. All the ordinary, decent-hearted reader will ask is that the transformation be astonishing and interesting and that the story in some way appear to make sense, keep us reading. Or the writer may use a cast of clown characters—eagerly heroic nitwits like the Keystone Cops, or fiendish daemonic plotters with heads full of straw, like the Marx Brothers stealing a piano, etc. Where plot is concerned, anything can happen that wants to, so long as it holds interest; and setting may change as whimsically as it did from panel to panel in the *Krazy Kat* comics. Jazzing around may cover anything from parody to whimsey to heavy European surrealism. Unfortunately, it is what most beginning writers do most of the time; that is, they start with some character for whom they feel some sort of affection—an electric-guitar player, say—and they describe him playing his guitar in his room, and then they ask themselves, "Now what can I make happen?" Something dreary occurs to them—the guitar player's roommate comes in—and they write it down. The roommates smoke some pot. They go to a party. They meet a girl with a large white wolf. And so on. All of which is to say: Jazzing around is the hardest kind of fiction in the world. When a writer is good at it, the world is his—what's the expression?—*oyster?*

Yet in the end, alas, the world's greater praise will go to the serviceable drudge who writes about more or less lifelike people who, laboring through energeic plots, find their destinies and stir us to affirmation.

Metafiction, deconstructive fiction, and jazzing around all have this much in common with conventional fiction: They all delight us, or, as Nabokov used to insist, "charm." Whether a given work is boisterous, like a circus, or quietly elegant, like a sailboat, or disorienting, like an unpleasant dream come alive, or something else, all good fiction has moment-by-moment fascination. It has authority and at least a touch of strangeness. It draws us in. In the case of what I've called conventional fiction, it's easy to describe the basis of our attraction. For unconventional fiction, that is not so. Mystery is its soul. Sometimes when we look closely at an unconventional piece of fiction, we discover that in fact it's a simple achievement of genre-crossing—for instance, the folktale and the early Hollywood murder mystery—but we may be discovering more than the writer knew. As we've seen, conventional fiction takes immensely careful planning if it's to be really good, and metafiction and deconstructive fiction take similar care. Jazzing around takes a special genius, in which the ability to plan plays hardly any part. It requires inexhaustible imagination (think of the work of Stanley Elkin, for instance) and the taste to know when the magic isn't quite good enough. The two gifts, one extraordinarily childlike, the other highly sophisticated and mature, almost never show up in one person. Occasionally they show up in two, as in Gilbert and Sullivan, and the two fight like devils.

II

NOTES ON
THE FICTIONAL PROCESS

5

Common Errors

The most important single notion in the theory of fiction I have outlined—essentially the traditional theory of our civilization's literature—is that of the vivid and continuous fictional dream. According to this notion, the writer sets up a dramatized action in which we are given the signals that make us "see" the setting, characters, and events; that is, he does not tell us about them in abstract terms, like an essayist, but gives us images that appeal to our senses—preferably all of them, not just the visual sense— so that we seem to move among the characters, lean with them against the fictional walls, taste the fictional gazpacho, smell the fictional hyacinths. In bad or unsatisfying fiction, this fictional dream is interrupted from time to time by some mistake or conscious ploy on the part of the artist. We are abruptly snapped out of the dream, forced to think of the writer or the writing. It is as if a playwright were to run out on stage, interrupting his characters, to remind us that he has written all this. I am not saying that a novelist cannot noticeably treat his characters as puppets in a stage-set world, since puppets and a stage set are also things we can see and to some extent empathize with. Even the most "objective" fiction, as Robert Louis Stevenson called it, is still fiction, still dramatization.

If the principle of vividness and continuity is clear, we can turn to some technical implications.

A scene will not be vivid if the writer gives too few details to stir and guide the reader's imagination; neither will it be vivid if the language the writer uses is abstract instead of concrete. If the writer says "creatures" instead of "snakes," if in an attempt to impress us with fancy talk he uses Latinate terms like "hostile maneuvers" instead of sharp Anglo-Saxon words like "thrash," "coil," "spit," "hiss," and "writhe," if instead of the desert's sand and rocks he speaks of the snakes' "inhospitable abode," the reader will hardly know what picture to conjure up on his mental screen. These two faults, insufficient detail and abstraction where what is needed is concrete detail, are common—in fact all but universal—in amateur writing. Another is the failure to run straight at the image; that is, the needless filtering of the image through some observing consciousness. The amateur writes: "Turning, she noticed two snakes fighting in among the rocks." Compare: "She turned. In among the rocks, two snakes were fighting." (The improvement can of course be further improved. The phrase "two snakes were fighting" is more abstract than, say, "two snakes whipped and lashed, striking at each other"; and verbs with auxiliaries ["were fighting"] are never as sharp in focus as verbs without auxiliaries, since the former indicate indefinite time, whereas the latter [e.g., "fought"] suggest a given instant.) Generally speaking—though no laws are absolute in fiction—vividness urges that almost every occurrence of such phrases as "she noticed" and "she saw" be suppressed in favor of direct presentation of the thing seen.

The technical implications of the continuity principle—the idea that the reader should never be distracted from the image or scene—cannot be treated so briefly. In the work of beginning writers, especially those weak in the basic skills of English composition, the usual mistake is that the writer distracts the reader by clumsy or incorrect writing. Characters, of course, can speak as clumsily as they like; the writer's job is simply to imitate them accurately. But the standard third-person narrator can never miss. If the narrator slips into faulty syntax, the reader's mind tacks away from the fighting snakes to the problem of figuring out what the sentence means. The distraction is almost certain to be emotional as well as intellectual, since the reader has every right to feel that the writer's business is to say what he means clearly. In good fiction, the reader never has to go back over a sentence just to find out what it says. He may read a sentence twice because he likes it, or because, through no fault of the author, his mind briefly wandered, musing, perhaps, on the larger implications of the scene; but if it's the author's carelessness that makes him read twice, he has a right to feel that the author has violated the fundamental contract in all fiction: that the writer will deal honestly and responsibly with the reader. (This, it should be mentioned, does not rule out use of the so-called unreliable narrator, since the unreliable narrator is a character inside the fiction.)

Clumsy writing is an even more common mistake in the work of amateurs, though it shows up even in the work of very good writers. Some of the more frequent forms of clumsy writing should perhaps be mentioned here, since faults of this kind are a good deal more serious than the amateur may imagine. They alienate the experienced reader, or at very least make it hard for him to concentrate on the fictional dream, and they undercut the writer's authority. Where lumps and infelicities occur in fiction, the sensitive reader shrinks away a little, as we do when an interesting conversationalist picks his nose.

The most obvious forms of clumsiness, really failures in the basic skills, include such mistakes as inappropriate or excessive use of the passive voice, inappropriate use of introductory phrases containing infinite verbs, shifts in diction level or the regular use of distracting diction, lack of sentence variety, lack of sentence focus, faulty rhythm, accidental rhyme, needless explanation, and careless shifts in psychic distance. Let us run through these one by one.

Except in stock locutions, such as "You were paid yester-
day," "The Germans were defeated," or "The project was abandoned," the passive voice is virtually useless in fiction except
when used for comic effect, as when the writer mimics some
fool's slightly pompous way of speaking or quotes some institu-
tional directive. The active voice is almost invariably more direct and vivid: "Your parrot bit me" as opposed to (passive) "I
was bitten by your parrot." (The choice in this case may depend
on characterization. A timid soul fearful of giving offense might
well choose the passive construction.) In a story presented by
the conventional omniscient narrator—an objective and largely
impersonal formal narrative voice like, say, Tolstoy's—the passive voice is almost certain to offend and distract. Needless to
say, the writer must judge every case individually, and the really good writer may get away with just about anything. But
it must be clear that when the writer makes use of the passive
he knows he's doing it and has good reason for what he does.

Sentences beginning with infinite-verb phrases are so common in bad writing that one is wise to treat them as guilty until
proven innocent—sentences, that is, that begin with such
phrases as "Looking up slowly from her sewing, Martha said . . ."
or "Carrying the duck in his left hand, Henry . . ." In really
bad writing, such introductory phrases regularly lead to shifts in
temporal focus or to plain illogic. The bad writer tells us, for
instance: "Firing the hired man and burning down his shack,
Eloise drove into town." (The sentence implies that the action
of firing the hired man and burning down his shack and the
action of driving into town are simultaneous.) Or the bad writer
tells us, "Quickly turning from the bulkhead, Captain Figg
spoke slowly and carefully." (Illogical; that is, impossible.) But
even if no illogic or confusion of temporal focus is involved, the
too frequent or inappropriate use of infinite-verb phrases makes
bad writing. Generally it comes about because the writer cannot
think of a way to vary the length of his sentences. The writer
looks at the terrible thing he's written: "She slipped off the

garter. She turned to John. She smiled at his embarrassment," and in a desperate attempt to get rid of the dully thudding subjects and verbs he revises to "She slipped off the garter. Turning to John, she smiled at his embarrassment." The goal, sentence variety, may be admirable, but there are better ways. One can get rid of the thudding subjects and verbs by using compound predicates: "She slipped off the garter and turned to John"; by introducing qualifiers and appositional phrases: "She slipped—or, rather, yanked—off the garter, a frayed, mournful pink one long past its prime, gray elastic peeking out past the ruffles, indifferently obscene" (etc.); or by finding some appropriate subordinate clause, perhaps: "When she had slipped off the garter, she turned to John"—a solution that gets rid of the thudding by lowering (hastening) the stress of the first "she." (Compare the two rhythms: "She slipped off the garter. She turned to John" and "When she had slipped off the garter, she turned to John.") All this is not to deny, of course, that the introductory infinite-verb phrase can be an excellent thing in its place. Properly used, it momentarily slows down the action, gives it a considered, weighted quality that can heighten the tension of an important scene. It works well, for instance, in situations like these: "Slowly raising the rifle barrel . . ." or "Gazing off at the woods, giving her no answer . . ." Used indiscriminately, the introductory infinite-verb phrase chops the action into fits and starts and loses what effectiveness it might have had, properly set.

Diction problems are usually symptomatic of defects in the character or education of the writer. Both diction shifts and the steady use of inappropriate diction suggest either deep-down bad taste or the awkwardness that comes of inexperience and timidity. There seems little or no hope for the adult writer who produces sentences like these: "Her cheeks were thick and smooth and held a healthy natural red color. The heavy lines under them, her jowls, extended to the intersection of her lips and gave her a thick-lipped frown most of the time." The phrase

"Her cheeks were thick and smooth" is normal English, but "[Her cheeks] held a healthy natural red color" is elevated, pseudo-poetic. The word "held" faintly hints at personification of "cheeks," and "healthy natural red color" is clunky, stilted, slightly bookish. The second sentence contains similar mistakes. The diction level of "extended to the intersection of her lips" is high and formal, in ferocious conflict with the end of the sentence, which plunges to the colloquial "most of the time." There may be slightly more hope for the writer who uses steadily elevated diction—sentences that pomp along like these: "The unique smell of urine and saltwater greeted him as he stepped through the hatchway. He surveyed the area for an open sink or shower stall but, finding none, had to wait in line." ("Had to wait in line" is of course a sudden diction drop.) The writing here has most of the usual qualities of falsely elevated diction: abstract language ("unique smell"), cliché personification ("[the smell] greeted him"), Latinate language where simple Anglo-Saxon would be preferable ("surveyed the area" for "looked around"), and so forth. If a writer with difficulties like these sticks to the relatively easy kinds of fiction—the realistic story and the yarn as opposed to the tale—he can get rid of his problems simply. He can learn by diligence to eradicate all traces of fancy talk from his vocabulary, using direct, colloquial speech in realistic stories and in yarns imitating the conventional backwater narrative voice (the rural Southerner, the crafty old farmer of New England, or whatever). Serious tales, which by convention require elevated, almost stately tone, are likely to prove forever beyond this writer's means, since no one can write in the high style if he cannot tell real high style from fake. It's a limitation no writer should happily accept, as a few phrases from Melville should remind us:

The morning was one peculiar to that coast. Everything was mute and calm, everything grey. The sea, though undulated into long roods of swells, seemed fixed, and was sleeked at the surface like waved lead that has cooled and set in the smelter's mould. The sky seemed a grey mantle. Flights of troubled grey fowl, kith and kin with flights of troubled grey vapours among which they were mixed, skimmed low and fitfully over the waters, as swallows over meadows before storms. Shadows present, foreshadowing deeper shadows to come.

Or look at an example of Isak Dinesen's use of the tale's traditional high style:

> The big house stood as firmly rooted in the soil of Denmark as the peasants' huts, and was as faithfully allied to her four winds and her changing seasons, to her animal life, trees and flowers. Only its interests lay in a higher plane. Within the domain of the lime trees it was no longer cows, goats, and pigs on which the minds and the talk ran, but horses and dogs. The wild fauna, the game of the land, that the peasant shook his fist at when he saw it on his young green rye or in his ripening wheat field, to the residents of the country houses were the main pursuit and the joy of existence.
>
> The writing in the sky solemnly proclaimed continuance, a worldly immortality. The great country houses had held their ground through many generations. The families who lived in them revered the past as they honoured themselves, for the history of Denmark was their own history.

The high style, like Bach, is not for everyone; but the fact that amateurs so regularly fall into grotesque imitation of it suggests that it strikes some responsive chord in us. By reading carefully and extensively, by writing constantly and getting the best criticism available to him, the writer who begins with no feeling for diction can eventually overcome his problems.

Sentence variety is discussed in most freshman composition

books and need not be treated at length here; it will be enough
to mention one or two of the problems that most frequently
plague creative writers. What the young writer needs to do, of
course, is study sentences, consciously experiment with them,
since he can see for himself what the difficulty is, and can see
for himself when he has beaten it: Where variety is lacking,
sentences all run to the same length, carry over and over the
same old rhythms, and have the same boring structure. Subject-
verb, subject-verb, subject-verb-object, subject-verb. What the
alert writer learns as he begins to experiment is that the cure
can be worse than the disease. I've mentioned already the usually ill-fated introduction of an opening infinite-verb phrase.
Another bad cure is the sentence awkwardly stretched out by a
"that" or "which" clause. For example, "Leaping from the couch,
he seized the revolver from the bookshelf that stood behind the
armchair," or, "She turned, shrieking, throwing up her arms in
terror at the sight of the gorilla that had arrived that morning
from Africa, which had formerly been its home." What happens
in such sentences, obviously, is that they tend to trail off, lose
energy. It may help to look at the matter this way: Sentences in
English tend to fall into meaning units or syntactic slots—for
instance, such patterns as

$$\overset{1}{\text{subject,}} \quad \overset{2}{\text{verb,}} \quad \overset{3}{\text{object}}$$

or

$$\overset{1}{\text{subject,}} \quad \overset{2}{\text{verb-modifier.}}$$

In the so-called periodic sentence, highly recommended by highschool English teachers, the most interesting or important thing
in the sentence is pushed into the final slot, as in "Down the
river, rolling and bellowing, came Mabel's cow." The natural
superiority of the periodic sentence can be exaggerated, but it is
a fact that an anticlimactic ending can ruin an otherwise perfectly good sentence, and almost invariably—except in comic

writing—the "that" or "which" clause leads to anticlimax. (In *New Yorker* "super-realist" fiction, this stylistic flatness may be a virtue.)

Often the search for variety leads to another problem, the overloading of sentences and the loss of focus. Look at these sentences: "The dark waters of the Persian Gulf were very peaceful as the pinkish glow of pre-dawn light turned the horizon's gray clouds to shades of orchid and lavender. The clear, cool air breezed across the decks of the mammoth white ship as it moved almost silently through the water." In a somewhat frantic attempt to get gusto, the writer packs his sentence like a Japanese commuter train. Perhaps a great writer might get away with this (in prose fiction Dylan Thomas and Lawrence Durrell have tried it), but it seems not too likely. As a rule, if a sentence has three syntatic slots, as in

$$\overset{1}{\text{The }} \overset{2}{\text{man walked}} \overset{3}{\text{down the road}}$$

—a writer may load one or two of the slots with modifiers, but if the sentence is to have focus—that is, if the reader is to be able to make out some clear image, not just a jumble—the writer cannot cram all three syntactic slots with details. So, for instance, the writer may load down slot 1 and leave the others more or less alone, thus:

> 1
> The old man, stooped, bent almost double under his load of tin pans, yet smiling with a sort of maniacal good cheer and chattering to himself in what seemed to be Slavonian,
> 2   3
> walked slowly down the road.

Or he may load up slot 2:

> 1   2
> The old man walked slowly, lifting his feet carefully, sometimes kicking one shoe forward in what looked like

a dance, then slamming down the foot before the sole
could flop loose again, grinning when it worked, mutter-

3

ing to himself, making no real progress down the road.

Or the writer may risk piling high precarious loads on both slots
1 and 2; for instance:

1

The old man, stooped, bent almost double under his load
of tin pans, yet smiling with a sort of maniacal good cheer
and chattering to himself in what seemed to be Slavonian,

2

walked slowly, lifting his feet carefully, sometimes kicking one shoe forward in what looked like a dance, then
slamming down the foot before the sole could flop loose
again, grinning when it worked, pleased with himself, but

3

making no real progress down the road.

If what chiefly interests him is literary stunts (and such things
are not all bad, though they can detract from fiction's seriousness), the writer can oonch slot 3 just a little, changing it in the
sentence above to something like "the bumpy, crooked road."
This sort of playing around with sentences is one of the chief
things that make writing a pleasure; nevertheless, no writer can
help but recognize that eventually enough is enough.

Readers sensitive to the virtues of good fiction can be distracted from the fictional dream by subtler kinds of mistakes.
One of these is faulty rhythm. Many writers, including some
famous ones, write with no consciousness of the poetic effects
available through prose rhythm. They put the wine on the table,
put the cigarette in the ashtray, paint in the lovers, start the
clock ticking, all with no thought of whether the sentences
should be fast or slow, light-hearted or solemn with wedged-in
juxtaposed stresses. I am not speaking now of the intentionally
arhythmic writer, the kind who never allows himself a passage

that stands out as rhythmically beautiful but on the other hand
never makes us stumble or dance for our footing like a calf on
ice. In realistic fiction, such writers argue, an important part of
the writer's business is to imitate the way real people speak; and
since in life people do not generally speak in fine poetic
rhythms, the controlling narrator, who must thread the rhythms
of his speech in with the rhythms of the characters, is wise to
keep his rhythms unnoticeable; wise, that is, to steer as far as
possible from the rhythms of bardic or incantatory writers like
James Joyce, Thomas Wolfe, or William Faulkner. To choose
the bardic voice is automatically to take a slight step back from
realism, to move from the casually spoken to the intoned, from
the realistic story toward the tale. Both the intentionally
arrhythmic writer—John Updike is an example—and the writer,
like myself, who would sacrifice a character's ears for melodic
effect, can be counted on not to distract the reader from his
dream by clunky rhythms. The writer who simply never thinks
about rhythm is almost certain to do so. The reader may suddenly be stopped cold by a line in accidental doggerel:

> / ˘ ˘ / ˘ ˘ / ˘ ˘ / ˘ ˘
> No one was looking when Tarkington's gun went off,
> / ˘ ˘ / ˘ ˘ / ˘ ˘ /
> killing James Harris and maiming his wife.*

The writer thus unintentionally produces a form of sprung verse
—that is, jammed stresses one after another—when what he
needs, to reflect the moment's rush, is lighter rhythms, anapests
or dactyls. For example, he may write:

> / / / / / / / / /
> "Stop, thief!" Bones Danks cried. "Stop! Can't some good
> / / / / /
> soul stop that man, please?"

Needless to say, the writer who does pay attention to rhythm
can also find ways of distracting the reader from the fictional

* For explanation of the metrical markings, see pp. 150–51.

dream, mainly by overdoing things—that is, by letting his ego get in the way of his materials—but this we need not speak of now, since we will need to look later at Longinus' principle of frigidity.

Another irritant is accidental rhyme, as in the sentence "When the rig blew, everything went flying sky-high—me too." Notice here that the rhyme is offensive because both rhyme-words, "blew" and "too," are stressed positions; that is, the voice comes down hard on them. The rhyme is not offensive, to most ears, if the writer can get one of the rhymes out of stressed position: "The rig blew sky-high, and everything went flying—me too." In this version the word "blew" gives away stress to "sky-high," and the "blew-too" rhyme drops toward background effect. Now, however, we have a new stressed rhyme—"sky-high" and "flying" (well, close enough for rhyme in prose)—and we notice an odd thing: It sounds OK. If we analyze the sounds, trying to understand the reason, we perhaps come up with this: First, the two-element rhyme "sky-high," with a hovering stress (see analysis below), is resolved by a feminine rhyme (a word ending with an unstressed syllable) followed by a phrase, "me too," that functions as a pull-away; the result is that the rhyme-word "flying" hits lightly in comparison with the rhyme base "sky-high," the voice hurrying on to the pull-away.

"The rig blew sky-high, and everything went flying—me too." Second, the phrase "me too" faintly recalls the unstressed base "blew" and at the same time rhythmically recalls "sky-high," with the result that the "sky-high—flying" rhyme is slightly muted. Let us turn the sentence around one last time, this time suppressing "blew":

"The rig went flying, and everything shot sky-high—me too." If we mentally substitute "blew" for "shot," we see—or, rather, hear—at once that it won't do—an extremely heavy, awkward rhyme of the kind certain to distract the reader; that is, make him stop thinking of the images for a moment to wonder what's gone wrong with the writer's brain. On the other hand, with "shot," the "flying—sky-high" rhyme seems acceptable. The sentence's *andante* opening (loosely iambic) accelerates to its *allegro* mid-section ("flying, and everything"), and then suddenly the sentence opens out like a huge, slow firework, with repeated jammed stresses to balance the quickness earlier and the "sky-high" rhyme rising like a crown. This kind of poetic effect in fiction distracts only in an acceptable way. The reader may pause and read the sentence twice, savoring the way sound echoes sense, but if he has turned for a moment from the fictional dream it is only in the way we pause sometimes to admire the technique of an animal trainer—the flourish with which he lowers his head into the jaws of the crocodile—after which we throw ourselves back into watching the act. Writers very sure of their technical mastery—*tour-de-force* writers—may make a kind of game of seeing how far they can go, winking and leering at the reader, before breaking the fictional illusion. On that, more later.

Needless explanation and explanation where drama alone would be sufficient are other irritants. In amateur fiction these problems may show up in crude forms, but experienced writers can make mistakes of the same basic kinds. The amateur writer tells us, for instance, that Mrs. Wu is a crabby old woman and explains that one reason is Mrs. Wu's trouble with sciatica. All of this information could and should have been conveyed through dialogue and action. We should have seen her kicking the cat out of the way, rubbing her hip, yelling out the window at Mr. Chang, who's parked his truck on her curb. We should hear her on the telephone, complaining to her son in San Diego. Experienced writers can make the same mistake—usually, if not invariably, out of a too great fondness on the writer's part for the mellifluous tones of his own voice. He may write:

> Detective Gerald B. Craine was very drunk. Sitting
> that morning in the parked truck, he couldn't tell reality
> —or, at any rate, what you and I call reality—from the

shadows and phantoms produced by his delirium tremens. His sense of responsibility, his courage, his nobility of heart, his native chivalry, all these were as keen as ever; but his eye for mundane truth was not what it might have been. And so, believing he saw something, and thinking himself called upon for heroic action, he threw down the bottle, snatched out his revolver, ran into the house where the girl had just gone, and once again proved himself a fool.

Voice, once a writer masters it, can be a delightful thing, but no smart writer depends on voice alone to sail him past all evils. Compare another version of the scene with the drunken detective, this time dramatized, not explained:

Where the snake came from he did not see. A roar filled his mind, the sky flashed white, and as if the doorway to the underworld had opened, there lay the snake, a foot across, maybe thirty feet long, greenish-golden. It moved quickly, gracefully across the street in front of him and over the curb toward the porch where a moment ago Elaine Glass had stood. It had large black eyes; in its scales, glints of violet and vermillion. Hatchet-head raised, tongue flicking, it moved with the assurance of a familiar visitor up the sidewalk toward the steps.

With a yelp, without thinking, Craine threw down the bottle, pushed open the door of his side, half-jumped, half-fell from the truck, and ran around the front. He drew his pistol as he ran. The students on the porch snatched their things from the steps and porch-floor and jumped back. The tail of the enormous snake was disappearing through the door. Now it was gone. He ran after it, waving the pistol, running so fast he could hardly keep from falling.

Though we run across exceptions, philosophical novels where explanation holds interest, the temptation to explain is one that should almost always be resisted. A good writer can get anything at all across through action and dialogue, and if he can think of no powerful reason to do otherwise, he should probably leave explanation to his reviewers and critics. The writer should especially avoid comment on what his characters are feeling, or at very least should be sure he understands the common objection summed up in the old saw "Show, don't tell." The reason, of course, is that set beside the complex thought achieved by drama, explanation is thin gruel, hence boring. A woman, say, decides to leave home. As readers, we watch her all morning, study and think about her gestures, her mutterings, her feelings about the neighbors and the weather. After our experience, which can be intense if the writer is a good one, we *know* why the character leaves when finally she walks out the door. We know in a way almost too subtle for words, which is the reason that the writer's attempt to explain, if he's so foolish as to make the attempt, makes us yawn and set the book down.

Careless shifts in psychic distance can also be distracting. By psychic distance we mean the distance the reader feels between himself and the events in the story. Compare the following examples, the first meant to establish great psychic distance, the next meant to establish slightly less, and so on until in the last example, psychic distance, theoretically at least, is nil.

1. It was winter of the year 1853. A large man stepped out of a doorway.
2. Henry J. Warburton had never much cared for snowstorms.
3. Henry hated snowstorms.
4. God how he hated these damn snowstorms.
5. Snow. Under your collar, down inside your shoes, freezing and plugging up your miserable soul . . .

When psychic distance is great, we look at the scene as if from far away—our usual position in the traditional tale, remote in time and space, formal in presentation (example 1 above would appear only in a tale); as distance grows shorter—as the camera dollies in, if you will—we approach the normal ground of the yarn (2 and 3) and short story or realistic novel (2 through 5). In good fiction, shifts in psychic distance are carefully controlled. At the beginning of the story, in the usual case, we find the writer using either long or medium shots. He moves in a little for scenes of high intensity, draws back for transitions, moves in still closer for the story's climax. (Variations of all kinds are possible, of course, and the subtle writer is likely to use psychic distance, as he might any other fictional device, to get odd new effects. He may, for instance, keep a whole story at one psychic-distance setting, giving an eerie, rather icy effect if the setting is like that in example 2, an overheated effect that only great skill can keep from mush or sentimentality if the setting is like that in example 5. The point is that psychic distance, whether or not it is used conventionally, must be controlled.) A piece of fiction containing sudden and inexplicable shifts in psychic distance looks amateur and tends to drive the reader away. For instance: "Mary Borden hated woodpeckers. Lord, she thought, they'll drive me crazy! The young woman had never known any personally, but Mary knew what she liked."

Clumsy writing of the kinds I've been discussing cannot help distracting the reader from the dream and thus ruining or seriously impairing the fiction. I've limited myself to the most common kinds, or those that have proved most common in my experience as a writing teacher and sometime editor of books and literary magazines. Among very bad writers even worse faults appear—two or three spring immediately to mind and may as well be mentioned: getting the events in an action out of order, cloddishly awkward insertion of details, and certain persistent oddities of imitation or spelling difficult to account for except by a theory of activity by the Devil. The first of these should need no explanation. I refer simply to the presentation of a series of actions where by some means the writer—perhaps because his mind is focused on something else—gets events out of sequence, forcing the reader to go back and straighten them out; or, to put it another way, where the writer momentarily suspends meaning in his sentence (almost always a bad idea), forcing the reader to run on faith for several words, hoping that out of seeming chaos some sense will emerge. Two examples. First: "Turning, dribbling low as he went in for his shot, he was suddenly knocked flat by one of the cheerleaders, who had rushed onto the court in her excitement and so had gotten in his way." A sentence like this one can be fobbed off on the reader occasionally—though the sharp reader will notice and object—but if such things happen often the authority of the writer is seriously undermined and, more to the point, the dream loses power and coherence. If we are to see a perfectly focused dream image, we must be given the signals one by one, in order, so that everything happens with smooth logicality, perfect inevitability. The only exception (and even here the writer should be sure his exception is justified) is the scene in which the character's disorientation—and the reader's—is meant to be an important part of the effect. Bad writers use this exception as an excuse to introduce voices out of nowhere, as when we have a young man walking down the road, whistling happily, no one in sight, and then we encounter the words (new paragraph): " 'Watch yourself, Boon!' " Followed by (new paragraph): "Boon turned in alarm, looking all around in panic." This kind of thing is common in fiction, of course, and my disapproval will not do much to discourage writers from continuing to use it. Nevertheless, if the theory of fiction as a dream in the reader's mind is correct, the surprise break into the calm of things ("Watch yourself") is a mistake, or anyway a lapse from absolute, perfectly focused clarity. Compare: "Suddenly, from somewhere, a voice shouted, 'Watch yourself, Boon!' " But these are delicate matters, and every writer will have his own opinion on just how far he ought to go in pursuit of the ideal of clarity. As far as I'm concerned, if the writer has at least seriously *thought* about the problem and fully understands the advantages of keeping event *a* in front of event *b* and all the event chains as sensible and clear as falling dominoes, he can—and should—do whatever feels best to him. Who knows what's going on in the early novels of John Hawkes? And yet few writers have ever created more powerful and coherent dreams.

Practically nothing need be said, either, about the cloddishly awkward insertion of details. One thinks of those moments, so common in even professional fiction, when the writer finds himself struggling (as if for the first time) with the age-old problem of smoothly introducing the looks of his central character. (She happens past a mirror, sees her face in a clockface, happens on a friend who gushes about how she used to look as opposed to how she looks now; or the writer, throwing in the towel, just tells us, and the hell with it.) Any experienced writing teacher can give tips on how to slip things in with the dexterity of a magician forcing cards into the hand of his assistant from the audience, but really all that needs to be said—or ought to be said—is this: What the honest writer does, when he's finished a rough draft, is go over it and over it, time after time, refusing to let anything stay if it looks awkward, phony, or forced. Clumsily inserted details must either be revised into neatly inserted details or they must be revised out of the fiction.

As for the third of the amateur sins I mentioned, oddities of imitation or spelling, the less said the better. I mean things like, in dialogue, "um, uh . . ."—sometimes used by good writers in ways that don't stand out and distract from the fictional dream, but usually used by amateurs in ways that make the reader tear his hair. As long as one has a narrator available, one can avoid funny-looking dialogue by simply saying, for example, "Carlos said, stammering slightly, 'I don't know.' " (No need then for an "um" or a "d-d-d-don't.") And then there are odd spellings like "Yea" for "Yeah" or "Yeh," spellings whereby football players or drug pushers start sounding like Jesus ("Yea verily").

All of these clumsy kinds of writing belong under the heading "Learning the Basic Skills" and are matters so obvious to the experienced reader or writer that they seem at first glance to have no place in a book for serious writers. The reasons they do belong are, first, that the best writers do not always (or even often) come from the well-educated upper middle class—art's cauldron is only on rare occasions gold or silver—and, second, that clumsy errors of the kind I've been treating help show clearly what we mean when we speak of "things that distract the reader's mind from the fictional dream," and nothing in what I'm saying is more fundamental than the concept of the uninterrupted fictional dream.

Let us turn now to three faults far graver than mere clumsiness—not faults of technique but faults of soul: sentimentality, frigidity, and mannerism. Faults of soul, I've said; but I don't mean those words as a Calvinist would. Faults of soul, like faults of technique, can be corrected. In fact the main work a writing teacher does, and the main work the writer must do for himself, is bring about change in the writer's basic character, helping to make him that "true Poet," as Milton said, without whom there can be no true Poem.

Sentimentality, in all its forms, is the attempt to get some effect without providing due cause. (I take it for granted that the reader understands the difference between *sentiment* in fiction, that is, emotion or feeling, and *sentimentality*, emotion or feeling that rings false, usually because achieved by some form of cheating or exaggeration. Without sentiment, fiction is worthless. Sentimentality, on the other hand, can make mush of the finest characters, actions, and ideas.) The theory of fiction as a vivid, uninterrupted dream in the reader's mind logically requires an assertion that legitimate cause in fiction can be of only one kind: drama; that is, character in action. Once it is dramatically established that a character is worthy of our sympathy and love, the story-teller has every right (even the obligation, some would say) to give sharp focus to our grief at the misfortunes of that character by means of powerful, appropriate rhetoric. (If the emotional moment has been well established, plain· statements may be just as effective. Think of Chekhov.) The result is strong sentiment, not sentimentality. But if the story-teller tries to make us burst into tears at the misfortunes of some character we hardly know; if the story-teller appeals to stock response (our love of God or country, our pity for the downtrodden, the presumed warm feelings all decent people have for children and small animals); if he tries to make us cry by cheap melodrama, telling us the victim that we hardly know is all innocence and goodness and the oppressor all vile black-heartedness; or if he tries to win us over not by the detailed and authenticated virtues of the unfortunate but by rhetorical clichés, by breathless sentences, or by superdramatic one-sentence paragraphs ("Then she saw the gun")—sentences of the kind favored by porno and thriller writers, and increasingly of late by supposedly serious writers—then the effect is sentimentality, and no reader who's experienced the power of real fiction will be pleased by it.

In great fiction we are moved by what happens, not by the whimpering or bawling of the writer's presentation of what happens. That is, in great fiction, we are moved by characters and events, not by the emotion of the person who happens to be telling the story. Sometimes, as in the fiction of Tolstoy or Chekhov—and one might mention many others—the narrative voice is deliberately kept calm and dispassionate, so that the emotion arising from the fictional events comes through almost wholly untinged by presentation; but restraint of that kind is not an aesthetic necessity. A flamboyant style like that of Faulkner at his best can be equally successful. The trick is simply that the style must work in the service of the material, not in advertisement of the writer. When the ideas, characters, and actions are firmly grounded, Thomas Wolfe's or William Faulkner's style can give fitting expression to a story's emotional content. Like the formal laments of a Greek chorus, great rolling waves of rhetoric can raise our joy or grief to a keen intensity that

transcends the mundane and takes on the richness and universality of ritual. What begins in the real, in other words, can be
uplifted by style to something we recognize, even as we read,
as at once the real and the real transmuted. So the passage on
the death of Joe Christmas, in *Light in August*, strikes the
reader as at once reality and artifice, fact and hymn. The prose
poetry, in all its majestic self-consciousness, its unabashed leap
above the language ordinary people really speak, causes us to
feel the resonance of the death and all it means. But it's because
the necessary drama has been presented—the lifelike causes laid
out in the story—that the rhetoric works. When Wolfe or
Faulkner works less carefully, as both sometimes do, trying to
make incantation substitute for character-in-action, the reader
squirms. We may squirm in the same way, it has often been
remarked, when we encounter the other extreme of manneristic
sentimentality, the whine we sometimes catch in Hemingway,
wherein understatement becomes a kind of self-pity.

The fault Longinus identified as "frigidity" occurs in fiction
whenever the author reveals by some slip or self-regarding intrusion that he is less concerned about his characters than he
ought to be—less concerned, that is, than any decent human
being observing the situation would naturally be. Suppose the
writer is telling of a bloody fistfight between an old man and his
son, and suppose that earlier in the story he has shown that the
old man dearly loves his son, though he can never find an
adequate way to show it, so that the son, now middle-aged, still
suffers from his belief that his father dislikes him, and wishes he
could somehow turn the old man's dislike to love. Suppose,
further, that the writer has established this story of misunder-
standings with sufficient power that when the fistfight begins—
the old man's blow to the side of his son's head, the son's aston-
ished raising of his arms for protection, the old man's second
blow, this time to the nose, so that the son in pain and fury hits
the old man on the ear—our reaction as we read is horror and
grief. We bend toward the book in fascination and alarm, and the

writer continues: "The old man was crying like a baby now and swinging wildly—harmlessly, now that he'd been hurt—swinging and crying, red-faced, like a baby with his diapers full." "Yuk!" we say, and throw the book into the fire. What has happened, of course, is that the writer has forgotten that his characters' situation is serious; he's responded to his own imagined scene with insufficient warmth, has allowed himself to get carried away by the baby image, and, momentarily forgetting or failing to notice the scene's *real* interest—the fact that a pathetic misunderstanding can have led to this—the writer snatches at (or settles for) a detail of, at best, trivial interest, dirty diapers. The writer lacks the kind of passion all true artists possess. He lacks the nobility of spirit that enables a real writer to enter deeply into the feelings of imaginary characters (as he enters deeply into the feelings of real people). In a word, the writer is frigid.

Strictly speaking, frigidity characterizes the writer who presents serious material, then fails to carry through—fails to treat it with the attention and seriousness it deserves. I would extend the term to mean a further cold-heartedness as well, the given writer's inability to recognize the seriousness of things in the first place, the writer who turns away from real feeling, or sees only the superficialities in a conflict of wills, or knows no more about love, beauty, or sorrow than one might learn from a Hallmark card. With the meaning thus extended, frigidity seems one of the salient faults in contemporary literature and art. It is sometimes frigidity that leads writers to tinker, more and more obsessively, with form; frigidity that leads critics to schools of criticism that take less and less interest in character, action, and the explicit ideas of the story. It may even be frigidity that steers the writer toward sentimentality, the faking of emotions the writer does not honestly feel. Frigidity is, in short, one of the worst faults possible in literature, and often the basis of other faults. When the amateur writer lets a bad sentence stand in his final draft, though he knows it's bad, the sin is frigidity:

He has not yet learned the importance of his art, the only art or science in the world that deals in precise detail with the causes, nature, and effects of ordinary and extraordinary human feeling. When a skillful writer writes a shallow, cynical, merely amusing book about extramarital affairs, he has wandered—with far more harmful effect—into the same unsavory bog.

Mannered writing seems at times a species of frigidity (Hemingway at his worst), at other times a species of sentimentality (Faulkner at his worst), but is best treated as a separate fault, since the mannered writer may be neither frigid nor sentimental but simply mannered. Mannered writing is writing that continually distracts us from the fictional dream by stylistic tics that we cannot help associating, as we read, with the author's wish to intrude himself, prove himself different from all other authors. The tics of mannered writing are not to be confused with stylistic devices that can be explained as clearly in the service of subject matter (character and action) or designed to express some new way of seeing (the special effects of some difficult but clearly justifiable style we must learn to tune in on, as we do to the styles of Gertrude Stein, Virginia Woolf, or, more recently, Peter Matthiessen in *Far Tortuga*). Neither should the tics of mannered writing be confused with those oddities we associate with inherent stiffness or nervousness, comparable to that of an amateur speaker who forms his sentences carefully and somewhat clumsily, as in the painstaking, sometimes clunky style of Sherwood Anderson. Look, for example, at the first two paragraphs of his "Death in the Woods."

She was an old woman and lived on a farm near the town in which I lived. All country and small-town people have seen such old women, but no one knows much about them. Such an old woman comes into town driving an old worn-out horse or she comes afoot carrying a basket. She may own a few hens and have eggs to sell. She brings them in a basket and takes them to a grocer. There she trades them in. She gets some salt pork and some beans. Then she gets a pound or two of sugar and some flour.

Afterward she goes to the butcher's and asks for some dog meat. She may spend ten or fifteen cents, but when she does she asks for something. In my day the butchers gave liver to anyone who wanted to carry it away. In our family we were always having it. Once one of my brothers got a whole cow's liver at the slaughter-house near the fairgrounds. We had it until we were sick of it. It never cost a cent. I have hated the thought of it ever since.

It's hard to believe that Anderson thinks country people talk this way, and the idea that he is imitating an illiterate man's way of writing is too discouraging to pursue. Yet, reading Anderson's carefully stiff work, we never get the sense that he writes as he does to call attention to himself. Either he *cannot* write more smoothly (but some of his fiction belies this) or else he writes in this farmerish way because the style expresses his fiction's purpose: It discourages us from looking for superficial beauty, the polish of entertainment, and encourages us to read him sobermindedly, with the sort of country earnestness that suits the plain, thoughtful narrator and his story. The style shows us not the writer's cleverness, much less his ego, but the tone and intention of his writing.

The tics of mannered writing, on the other hand, are those from which we gather, by the prickling of our thumbs, some ulterior purpose on the writer's part, a purpose perhaps not fully conscious but nevertheless suspect, putting us on our guard. Think of John Dos Passos at his most self-important, or George Bernard Shaw when he pontificates. Whereas the frigid writer lacks strong feeling, and the sentimental writer applies feeling indiscriminately, the mannered writer feels more strongly about his own personality and ideas—his ego, which he therefore keeps before us by means of style—than he feels about any of his characters—in effect, all the rest of humanity.

Mannered writing, then—like sentimentality and frigidity—arises out of flawed character. In critical circles it is considered bad form to make connections between literary faults and bad character, but for the writing teacher such connections are impossible to miss, hence impossible to ignore. If a male student writer attacks all womanhood, producing a piece of fiction that embarrasses the class, the teacher does less than his job requires if he limits his criticism to comments on the writer's excessive use of "gothic detail," the sentimentalizing tendency of his sentence rhythms, or the distracting effect of his heavily scatological diction. The best such timorous criticism can achieve is a revised piece of fiction that is free of all technical faults but no less embarrassing. To help the writer, since that is his job, the teacher must enable the writer to see—partly by showing him how the fiction betrays his distorted vision (as fiction, closely scrutinized, always will)—that his personal character is wanting.

Some writing teachers feel reluctant to do this kind of thing, and people who are not artists—people with no burning convictions about writing or the value of getting down to bedrock truth—are inclined to be sympathetic. Nobody's perfect, they generously observe. But the true artist is impatient with such talk. Circus knife-throwers know that it is indeed possible to be perfect, and one had better be. Perfection means hitting exactly what you are aiming at and not touching by a hair what you are not. It serves no useful purpose for the writer to remind himself that "even Homer sometimes nods." Homer doesn't, except in the most trivial ways; for instance, in his many long battle scenes, carelessly killing off the same soldier twice. Chaucer, in all his finest poems, achieves something very near perfection. Racine in *Phaedra*. Shakespeare in *Macbeth*. Serious critics sometimes argue that the standards in art are always relative, but all artistic masterpieces give them the lie. In the greatest

works of art—think of the last works of Cézanne or Beethoven—
there are no real mistakes. For this very reason (not snobbery or
malice) it is important to keep track of the faults of writers not
quite of the first rank, especially those writers close to our own
time, whose genius half-persuades us that their faults must
somehow be virtues.

When we look at writers of the last generation—to say nothing of the best-known writers now among us—no fault stands
out more visibly than mannered style. William Faulkner,
though one of the best of men and often a brilliant writer, was
highly mannered. One more "apotheosis," the reader feels, and
he'll be driven to blow up some church. In the late works, the
reader feels again and again that Faulkner is trying to recapture
lost successes by cranking up the rhetoric, originally invented to
convey ideas and emotions already present, but now mere steam
and roar and rattle, a freight train empty of its freight. Hemingway was as bad, though his mannered prose is antithetical to
Faulkner's. (Should anyone doubt that the Hemingway style is
excessively mannered, not just beautifully chiseled, as it is in
"The Snows of Kilimanjaro" and all his best short stories, let him
try reading through ten, fifteen stories in a row.) James Joyce
was another outrageous offender, as he knew himself. His lyrical
repetitions of key symbolic phrases, especially in *Ulysses*, can
never be explained fully by aesthetic function; they always
carry with them a hint of Joyce's dandyism, his middle-period
unwillingness to stand back from the work of art—as he himself
told the world it should do—his unwillingness as an artist to
imitate God, sitting "outside, indifferent, paring his nails." Late
in life, Joyce was enormously pained and frustrated by the
wrong turn he believed his career had taken after *Dubliners* and
Portrait. The finest short story ever written, he claimed, was
Tolstoy's late, simple little fable, "How Much Land Does a Man
Need?" That opinion, like other of Joyce's last opinions, is generally taken not too seriously. Joyce was ill, alcoholic, full of self-
hatred; he had recently created—and was still working over—

one of the towering works of the human mind and spirit, *Finnegans Wake*.

But while we're obviously right to keep Joyce's dissatisfaction with *Finnegans Wake* in perspective, we need to notice that in fact he said what he meant. He was pointing out, quite seriously, something that he'd discovered to be going wrong with the age—not only in his own work but in everybody's work. Turning back, with praise, to his early, most unmannered writings, and raising for inspection as a literary touchstone an unmannered, simple fable, Joyce was reiterating principles he had recognized from the beginning, though he'd slipped from them sometimes in practice. He'd said long ago that all fiction should begin "Once upon a time . . ." and by an ingenious trick had begun his *Portrait of the Artist* on that formula. He'd long since offered his memorable metaphor on the unobtrusive artist imitating God. He was pointing out, in short, an important truth, a truth his disciples both early and late, from Faulkner and Dos Passos forward, have too often refused to hear.

Not all original or strikingly individual writing is mannered. No style is easier to recognize than Chekhov's, but it's difficult to think of a writer less mannered. It should be clear, too, that though a writer may be painfully mannered in one place, he may not be in others. Nowhere in Joyce's finest work—"The Dead," for instance—do we find the artist's personality illegitimately intruding on the story. Nowhere in Melville's greatest passages, certainly not in "Benito Cereno" or "Bartleby the Scrivener," does Melville's voice rise to (as Lawrence said) a "bray." In these works, and others like them, poetic effects are kept subtle and unobtrusive. No one can fail to notice the poetic beauty of Joyce's closing lines in "The Dead," but the poetry comes from the rhythm of the sentences (rhythm so subtle only prose can achieve it), from the precisely focused imagery (the image of falling snow, which circles outward till it fills all the universe), and the last lines' echoes—merest whispers—of passages encountered earlier. Yet it need not be obvious poetic effect that makes a story seem mannered. As William Gass shows in his best fiction—"In the Heart of the Heart of the Country," for instance—even quite spectacular artifice can sit firmly inside the fiction, not suggesting intrusion by the writer.

What does the beginning writer look for, then, as signs that his writing is slipping toward the mannered? He should think hard about any innovation he's introduced into his work, making sure that the work would not be, for all practical purposes, the same if he had done what he's done in more conventional ways. So, for instance, if he has substituted commas for periods in much of the story, trying for some subtle new rhythmical effect that seems to him appropriate to this particular narrative, he might try retyping key passages in conventional punctuation, then reading both versions over and over, making sure that the new way really does add more than it detracts. (Detracts in the sense that it distracts the reader's mind until he adjusts to it—adjusts as we do to the best innovative writings.)

If the writer has introduced flamboyant poetic effects—noticeable rhyme, for example—the writer might read and re-read what he's written, then put it away awhile, allowing it to cool, then again read and reread, carefully analyzing his emotion as he reads, trying to make out whether the new device works because it gives new interest and life to the material or whether, on the other hand, it begins to wear thin, feel slightly creepy. Needless to say, no final decision, in a matter like this, should be based on cowardice. Any fool can revise until nothing stands out as risky, everything feels safe—and dead. One way or another, all great writing achieves some kind of gusto. The trick lies in writing so that the gusto is in the work itself, and whatever fire the presentation may have comes from the harmony or indivisibility of presentation and the thing presented.

6

Technique

What the young writer needs to develop, to achieve his goal of becoming a great artist, is not a set of aesthetic laws but artistic mastery. He cannot hope to develop mastery all at once; it involves too much. But if he pursues his goal in the proper way, he can approach it much more rapidly than he would if he went at it hit-or-miss, and the more successful he is at each stage along the way, the swifter his progress is likely to be. Invariably when the beginning writer hands in a short story to his writing teacher, the story has many things about it that mark it as amateur. But almost as invariably, when the beginning writer deals with some particular, small problem, such as description of a setting, description of a character, or brief dialogue that has some definite purpose, the quality of the work approaches the professional. This may not happen if the writer works blindly—if he has not been warned about the problems he will encounter and given some guidance on possible ways of dealing with the main problem set for him. But it's a common experience in writing classes that when the writer works with some sharply defined problem in technique, focusing on that alone, he produces such good work that he surprises himself. Success breeds success. Having written some small thing very well, he begins to learn confidence.

Two important lessons can be learned from the fact that the beginning writer does his best when working with some limited problem. The first is that the writer's relative indifference to his material can be an advantage (though this is by no means to say that the writer should always be indifferent to his material). In beginning an exercise assigned him by his teacher, the writer has no commitment to the message about to be conveyed, no concern about whether or not the character to be created is true to life—an accurate picture, say, of his mother. In an exercise, one simply makes things up as the assignment requires, and if by chance a talking tree emerges, one gets playfully involved in figuring out what a tree might think to mention. The tree, after all, must somehow be made interesting; otherwise the exercise will be a bore. In fact, the tree cannot help but say things of importance to the writer—otherwise the writer wouldn't have thought of the tree's remarks—and soon the writer discovers that his playful involvement has turned somewhat earnest. Consciously or not, he is expressing more feeling about, for instance, childhood frustrations and maternal love than he would be likely to spring in a true-to-life story about his mother. Whether a given exercise leads to realistic fiction or non-realistic fiction, it leads to fiction: to a studied simulation, through recollection and imaginative projection, of real feeling within the writer. When one writes about an actual parent, or friends, or oneself, all one's psychological censors are locked on, so that frequently, though not always, one produces either safe but not quite true emotion or else—from the writer's desire to tell the truth, however it may hurt—bold but distorted, fake emotion. In the first case, one's old friend Alma Spire, who was occasionally promiscuous, turns out to be "sensitive and warmly sensual"; in the second, she turns out to be a slut. Real-life characters do sometimes hold their own in fiction, but only those, loved or hated, whom the writer has transformed in his own mind, or through the process of writing, to imaginary beings. Writing an exercise, the writer is in the ideal artistic state, both serious and not serious. He wants the exercise to be wonderful, so that his class-mates will applaud, but he is not in the dark psychological set of the ambitious young novelist struggling to write down his exis-tence as it is, with the ghost of the young James Joyce standing horribly at his back.

Writing an exercise, the beginning writer is doing exactly what the professional does most of the time. Much of what goes into a real story or novel goes in not because the writer desper-ately wants it there but because he needs it: The scene justifies some later action, shows some basis of motivation, or reveals some aspect of character without which the projected climax of the action would not seem credible. Again and again one finds oneself laboriously developing some minor character one would never have introduced were he not needed to sell the clock for the time-bomb or to shear the sheep. Again and again one finds oneself struggling with all one's wits to make a thunderstorm vivid, not because one cares about thunderstorms but because, if the storm is not made real, no one will believe Martha's phonecall in the middle of the night. If he brilliantly succeeds with his exercise, the writer learns, consciously or not, the value of the mind-set that produced the success.

The second important lesson the beginning writer learns is that fiction is made of structural units; it is not one great rush. Every story is built of a number of such units: a passage of description, a passage of dialogue, an action (Leonard drives the pickup truck to town), another passage of description, more dialogue, and so forth. The good writer treats each unit individ-ually, developing them one by one. When he's working on the description of Uncle Fyodor's store, he does not think about the hold-up men who in a moment will enter it, though he keeps them in the back of his mind. He describes the store, patiently, making it come alive, infusing every smell with Uncle Fyodor's emotion and personality (his fear of hold-up men, perhaps); he works on the store as if this were simply an exercise, writing as if he had all eternity to finish it, and when the description is perfect—and not too long or too short in relation to its function in the story as a whole—he moves on to his story's next unit. Thinking in this way, working unit by unit, always keeping in mind what the plan of his story requires him to do but refusing to be hurried to more important things (Aunt Nadia's hysteria when the gun goes off), the writer achieves a story with no dead spots, no blurs, a story in which we find no lapses of aesthetic interest.

One way to begin on the road to artistic mastery, then, is to work at the systematic development of fictional techniques. By techniques I mean, of course, ways of manipulating fictional elements. No book can treat all the techniques that exist or might exist—every writer invents new ones or uses old ones in new ways—but it will be useful to examine here in general terms the role technique plays in contemporary fiction, then to look, more or less at random, at a few technical matters that prove basic.

In contemporary fiction, technique is, on the whole, more self-conscious than ever before. Given any basic story situation—the murderer creeping through the bushes, Grandmother's conversion, the lovers' first kiss—the contemporary writer is likely to know more ways of handling the situation than did the writer of any former time. Whereas once it was common for writers to work always in some one basic style, contemporary writers may on occasion change so radically from story to story or novel to novel that we can hardly believe their productions are all by one hand. The reasons are of course not far to seek. For one thing, we have more models available to us. When Sir Thomas Malory wrote a mass battle scene, he had virtually no models. The result is that, brilliant as he was as an innovator, his battles sound to modern ears tiresomely alike. The modern writer has a vast supply of available models, from Homer's writings to Mongolian bandit legends to stories from the French Revolution or Vietnam.

For another thing, thanks partly to certain movements in modern philosophy, the art of fiction, like all the arts, has become increasingly self-conscious and self-doubting, artists repeatedly asking themselves what it is they're doing. Chekhov and Tolstoy could say with great confidence that the business of fiction was "to tell the truth." Contemporary thought, as we've seen, is often skeptical about whether telling the truth is possible. Though we may be fairly confident that art does tell the truth, that fiction's elements and techniques form a language that the artist can use with great precision, and that the reader has intuitive means of checking on the truth of what the artist says, it will be helpful to look at this whole matter in a little more detail, since knowledge of the arguments will help clarify the role of technique.

Telling the truth in fiction can mean one of three things: saying that which is factually correct, a trivial kind of truth, though a kind central to works of verisimilitude; saying that which, by virtue of tone and coherence, does not feel like lying, a more important kind of truth; and discovering and affirming moral truth about human existence—the highest truth of art. This highest kind of truth, we've said, is never something the artist takes as a given. It's not his point of departure but his goal. Though the artist has beliefs, like other people, he realizes that a salient characteristic of art is its radical openness to persuasion. Even those beliefs he's surest of, the artist puts under pressure to see if they will stand. He may have a pretty clear idea where his experiment will lead, as Dostoevsky did when he sent Raskolnikov on his unholy mission; but insofar as he's a true artist, he does not force the results. He knows to the depths of his soul that when an artist creates in the service of wrong beliefs—that is, out of wrong opinions he mistakes for knowledge—or when he creates in the service of doctrines that may or may not be true but cannot be tested—for instance, doctrinaire Marxism or belief in the eventual resurrection of the dead—the effect of his work, admirable or otherwise, is not the effect of true art but of something else: pedagogy, propaganda, or religion.

But there remains one question, a central concern in all serious modern art, as in contemporary science; namely, the implications of the Heisenberg principle: To what extent does the instrument of discovery change the discovery, whether the instrument be "the process of fiction" or the particle bombardment of an atom?

Just as an anthropologist's presence among the group he is studying can alter the behavior of the group, or as the bombarding of an atom alters the pattern it means to illuminate, so the style in which an artist explores reality may alter the thing explored. Anyone can discern that, in music, emotion explored tonally differs from emotion explored atonally; and though it's impossible to prove that the generating emotions in the consciousness of the composer were in any way similar in the two cases, composers themselves have often expressed the opinion that having first chosen the musical form, one then bends one's thought to it, exactly as, having committed oneself to the key of D minor, one adapts the generative emotion to the resonance of that key; one would have said something different in the "happier" key of G major.

A few years ago, or so I've been told, a group of sound technicians conducted an experiment to discover whether they could heighten the "presence" of recorded music by multiplying tracks and speakers. The result was quadraphonic sound, but on the way to that result a strange thing occurred. A group of composers, musical performers, and critics were assembled to listen to music designed for four speakers, then eight speakers, then more. When listening to music on eight speakers, some of the musicians noted that what they were getting was not more accurate representation of music as we hear it in a hall but something quite new and different: One began to be able to locate the sounds in space. The clarinet seemed to occupy a particular point or area in the room, the trumpet another area, the piano another—not areas correspondent to the seating of the group recorded but areas related as the head, arms, and legs of a sculpture might be related. The music, in short, had become visual, something new under the sun. Writing music for eight speakers, a composer might theoretically shape music—physically shape it—as no one had ever done before. Whether or not any composer has explored that possibility I do not know, but the story, if it is true, illustrates a fact well known among artists, that art does not imitate reality (hold the mirror up to nature) but creates a new reality. This reality may be apposite to the reality we walk through every day—streets and houses, mailmen, trees—and may trigger thoughts and feelings in the same way a newly discovered thing of nature might do—a captured Big Foot or Loch Ness monster—but it is essentially itself, not the mirror reflection of something familiar.

The increasingly sharp recognition that art works in this way has generated the popularity, in recent years, of formalist art— art for art's sake—and metafiction, of which we spoke earlier. The general principle of the former has been familiar for centuries. The first modern thinker to define the mode clearly may have been Robert Louis Stevenson in his preface to the Chesterfield edition of the translated *Works of Victor Hugo*. There Stevenson pointed out that all art exists on a continuum between poles he calls "objective" and "subjective." At one extreme, the subjective, we have novels like those of Hugo, wherein we feel as we read that we are among the French mobs, surrounded by noise and smoke, transported from the room in which we read to Hugo's imaginary Paris. At the other extreme we have Fielding's *Tom Jones*, wherein we are never allowed to imagine for long that the hero is a "real" young man. As soon as we begin to incline to that persuasion, Fielding introduces a Homeric simile, or an interchapter, or something from the tradition of puppeteering, forcing us once more to recognize the novel as an object, not "real life." By way of illustration from the visual arts, Stevenson compares the effect of early- and middle-period Turner, when Turner landscapes were like vivid scenes seen through a window, and, on the other hand, the work of some unnamed French painter (one suspects that Stevenson may have made him up) who pasted real sand on his beach-scape in order that no one should mistake what he's looking at for a real beach on which a family might arrive to spread its picnic.

All literary parodists are inescapably creators of objective, or formalist, art. The parody becomes meaningless the moment we forget that the work is a literary object jokingly or seriously commenting on another literary object. In ordinary "realistic" fiction—what Stevenson would call subjective fiction—the writer's intent is that the reader fall through the printed page into the scene represented, so that he sees not words and fictional conventions but the dream image of, say, a tumbleweed crossing Arizona. In formalist fiction we are conscious mainly of the writer's art, or of both the tumbleweed and the art that makes it tumble. Excellent contemporary examples might be drawn from the fiction of William Gass but to save going and looking something up, I will use one from my own work. In my novella "The King's Indian" I parody, among other writers, Edgar Allan Poe. At one point I borrow directly from Poe: "My hair stood on end, my blood congealed, and I sank again into the bilgewater." If my effort is successful, the reader both sees the image in his mind—less a realist's image than one drawn from nineteenth-century magazine illustration—and sees Poe grinning and waving from the wings.

In the nineteenth century, most writers, though not all, trusted their implements and presented fictions unapologetically mimetic of life. If a writer emphasized the cartoon or puppet-stage quality of his art, as did Dickens, Thackeray, and Stevenson, he did so not because he distrusted art's relevance to life but either because he felt more or less indifferent to that relevance or because he enjoyed pure artifice, as we still do. The same may be said of Homer, Dante, Chaucer, "Monk" Lewis, or Smollett. If pressed, they would probably have said that they believed art directly relevant to life, but they loved artifice. Think of *Tristram Shandy*. The work is of course a spoof, a send-up of the novel and of story-telling in general, but no one doubts that Sterne intended Uncle Toby to seem to us lifelike. Poe is, among writers in English, the great nineteenth-century exception. The sad disparity between life and art (art kills or transforms life) is both his favorite subject and the principle behind his invention of new fictional forms. (He was the inventor of such forms—as we know them now—as the detective story, the horror story, the pirate story, the doppelgänger story, the story-as-painting ["Landor's Cottage"], and the fiction that is all denouement ["The Cask of Amontillado"].) For Poe, as for his great French translator, art's relation to life was far from innocent. In "Ligeia" he suggests allegorically that in pursuit of the ideal, the "dream memory" of Platonic philosophy (the narrator's memory of his lost Ligeia), the artist murders actuality. In "The Fall of the House of Usher," the resurrection of the lost beauty—blood-stained and horribly battered when she appears —is helped along by the narrator's reading of an old romance. Again and again in Poe's psychological allegories, the artist does his work much as witches do theirs, by following ancient formulas, creating art's effects with the daemonic help of older works of art.

Twentieth-century writers, for whom Poe and his followers opened the way, often have no confidence that art has relevance to life. Like their colleagues in science and philosophy, they make much of the fact that "a change of style is a change of subject." They know that eight speakers do not bring us closer to the reality of the concert hall, but create a new actuality, and the tendency of the writers is to pursue not life but the new actuality, the invention. Hence the fashion of linguistic sculpture and "opaque language."

It is, as we've seen, this same nervous fascination with art's untrustworthy character that has led to the popularity of metafiction, the piece of fiction on the subject of making fiction. Some of the more interesting recent examples—some of the less boring—are William Gass's *Willie Master's Lonesome Wife*, Ron Sukenick's "What's Your Story?" and John Barth's "Life-Story." A central concern in all such fiction is the extent to which technique or medium may be art's sole message. One of the most elegant of recent American metafictions is John Barth's "Lost in the Funhouse," the story of a boy who goes to a funhouse with his older sister and her lover, a sailor. All that is moving and beautifully written in the story, by customary standards, Barth interrupts with comments from real or imagined manuals on the art of fiction. We like and affirm the story's unsophisticated lovers, responding to the beauty of the prose that represents them; but the constant interruption of that prose with comments on how effective prose is written makes us irritably conscious of the extent to which moving prose is not natural but achieved. As a result, we doubt our naive response to the lovers, as Barth intends us to. We share—as in ordinary fiction we are never meant to do—the doubts and problems of the artist, but also his pleasure in his work, and in doing so lose the innocence of our delight in the funhouse and the experience of the lovers. Like the bright younger brother, we get no real pleasure from the sensations of life's funhouse; we slip in to where the lovers are pulled and become "lost."

Barth is not claiming that masterful technique is a thing to be avoided but only that, if possible, once one has captured it one should keep it on its chain. On one hand, showy technique is thrilling, as much in a work of fiction as in the work of a brilliant trapeze artist or animal trainer. No one would ask that the master artist hide his abilities. On the other hand, cleverness can become its own end, subverting higher ends, as when style overshadows character, action, and idea. The question is whether the artist can ever hold a balance between subject and presentation. Perhaps it is in the nature of art that actuality must be murdered, as it is in "Ligeia," and that what art brings forth is not some higher reality but a blood-stained thing that, like Madeline Usher, can flicker with apparent life for only an instant before collapsing back to death.

One curious result of the current, though not exactly new, fascination with the altering effect of technique on subject matter is what L. M. Rosenberg has identified as "fictional super-realism." The aim of writers in this mode (Mary Robison, Laura Furman, Ann Beattie, and others) is identical to that of photo-realists in painting or the sculptural exact copyist Duane Hansen, to get down reality without the slightest modification by the artist. As a group, they reject what would ordinarily be called "interesting plot." In one typical story, a character inherits a house in Hoosick Falls, New York, goes there to live in it and fix it up, and has brief, seemingly inconsequential conversations with neighbors. Plot profluence is limited to the fact that time passes, progressing to a moment of slight emotional rise (usually signaled by the transformation of descriptive details to a full-fledged image, the objectification of an unstated, trivial emotion); the conventional division of narrative into organized scenes is scrupulously avoided; if some insight is awakened or emotion stirred, the fact is simply reported, like any other fact. The writer makes an effort to choose images with the disinterest of a camera, and wherever possible he suppresses or carefully undercuts words with emotive effect. As Rosenberg points out, the writer does not allow himself even such dialogue tags as "she hollered" or "he exclaimed"; even questions—such as "Where in hell is the salt?"—are tagged "she said." The writers seek to bring to perfection the scientific ideal of Zola or William Dean Howells, treating nothing in nature as unworthy of notice and nothing as more worthy of notice than anything else. H. D.

Raymond, commenting on super-realist visual artists, offers a modern version of the old scientific ideal. "In omitting ideology, sublimity, and morality from their vision they are sworn to a phenomenologist credo. They stare unblinkingly at what is 'really' out there, ignoring the mental constructs through which they are peering."

One objection to the credo is old and obvious: We simply do not believe that reality is what these writers (and painters) maintain it to be. The realism is not "lifelike" because it seems to us dead. We may even suspect in the writer's suppression of emotion a certain unwitting dishonesty. Certainly no one who looks at the paintings of Philip Pearlstein, with their strong frontal lighting and accurate but slightly cartoonish emphasis of features—"stupid paintings," he calls them—can deny a faint suspicion that Pearlstein feels an unacknowledged contempt for the human form, even when the paintings are of his daughters.

Even the composer who writes for eight speakers, producing visual music, is likely to do more than simply follow out the possibilities of some new actuality. His emotion selects one visual music as more interesting than another. The suppression of the artist's personality can be virtually total, as in the fictional super-realism of Robison, Furman, and Beattie, writers whose abnegation of individual style is so complete that, except under the closest scrutiny, we cannot tell one writer's work from another's; yet the very suppression of style is a style—an aesthetic choice, an expression of emotion.

An opposite response to the current fascination with the effect of technique on subject matter may be found in the work of a group of contemporary non-realistic movements— Kafkaesque expressionism, surrealism, and the formalist "ir-realism" of writers like Borges and Barthelme. At its most expressionistic this movement produces, for example, the *Tropisms* of Nathalie Sarraute. In one of the tropisms, Sarraute describes an encounter between a young woman and an earnest old gentleman. Their conversation is awkward and intense:

But he interrupted her: "England . . . Ah, yes, England
. . . Shakespeare, eh? Eh? Shakespeare. Dickens. I remember, by the way, when I was young, I amused myself
translating Dickens. Thackeray. Have you read Thackeray? Th . . .Th . . . Is that how they pronounce it? Eh?
Thackeray? Is that it? Is that the way they say it?"

He had grabbed her and was holding her entirely in his
fist. He watched her as she flung herself about a bit, as she
struggled awkwardly, childishly kicking her little feet in
the air, while maintaining a pleasant smile: "Why yes, I
think it's like that. . . ."

Here, as in some of the works of Kafka, particular details of
psychological reality are directly translated into physical reality. Technique is not suppressed but emphasized, yet no real
divorce of actuality and the expression of actuality is suggested.
Neither is there any real divorce between actuality and expression in surrealist fiction (Jerzy Kosinski, William Palmer, sometimes John Hawkes); the difference is that here the reality
imitated is, not in one or two details but in many, that of our
dreams. In this fiction (as sometimes in the conventional tale),
things happen as if at random; only coherent emotion gives order.
At other times—here as in Kafka's dream stories ("A Country
Doctor")—a progression of events carries an emotional charge
not at first fully explained by the events themselves. The presentation tends to be that of conventional realistic fiction; only the
subject matter has changed. As the critic and writer Joe David
Bellamy puts it:

In the early twentieth-century novel of consciousness
or modernist short fiction, we are *inside* a character (or
characters) looking out. In the world of the contemporary
superfictionist, we are most frequently inside a character
(or characters) looking *in*—or these inner phantasms are
projected outward, and in a sometimes frightening, sometimes comic reversal, the outside "reality" begins to look

more and more like a mirror of the inner landscape—
there is so little difference between the two.

So-called absurdist fiction offers another variation. In Eugène
Ionesco's play *Rhinoceros*, the people of a town begin changing,
one by one, into rhinoceroses—all but the narrator, who at the
end of the story wishes he could change into a rhinoceros but
can't, and possibly his girlfriend, who perhaps changes as the
others have done, and then again perhaps simply pines away of
loneliness and guilt and disappears. The characters' transformation into rhinoceroses cannot be explained expressionistically,
since some of those who change are rhinoceroslike (stubborn,
ferocious, incapable of reasoning) and others are not; and neither can the story be interpreted as a dream. If anything, the
transformations reflect the workings of an absurd universe to
which all human responses ("our own moral code," "our philosophy," "our irreplaceable system of values," "humanism," even
love) are inadequate. (The story is commonly interpreted as
having to do with the acceptance of Nazi fascism.)

Among the more interesting and various of the "irrealists," a
group of writers who work out of fictional convention, abandon-
ing the attempt to deal directly with reality, is Donald Barthelme. All his work, from *Snow White* to *The Dead Father*,
might be read as, among other things, a *tour-de-force* study in
literary (and visual) technique. His worldview, in all his fiction,
is essentially absurdist: Characters struggle with problems that
cannot be solved and either accept their fate or struggle on.
Except for the fact that superficially Barthelme's method is
comic, and the fact, also, that the pathos of Barthelme's stories
is always muted, the emotional effect of his work is the same one
we get from naturalist fiction, irony and pity. One of the things
that make his writing interesting is his seemingly limitless ability to manipulate techniques as modes of apprehension. It goes
without saying that, for Barthelme, they apprehend nothing: Reality is a place we cannot get to from here. (The short story

"City Life" is in part a parody of super-realist fiction.) Yet at his best Barthelme can juggle techniques in a way that does express emotion and an attitude toward life. Take, for example, his well-known story from the collection *City Life*, "Views of My Father Weeping."

The story combines literary parody and surrealism (normally conflicting modes, the first "objective," in Stevenson's terms, the other "subjective"), together with snippets of other modes and styles, to tell a non-realistic story of a son's attempt to understand and avenge his father's death. The story opens:

> An aristocrat was riding down the street in his carriage. He ran over my father.
>
> .
>
> After the ceremony I walked back to the city. I was trying to think of the reason my father had died. Then I remembered: he was run over by a carriage.
>
> .
>
> I telephoned my mother and told her of my father's death. She said she supposed it was the best thing. I too supposed it was the best thing. His enjoyment was diminishing. I wondered if I should attempt to trace the aristocrat whose carriage had run him down. There were said to have been one or two witnesses.

The materials (e.g., "an aristocrat") are those of the conventional tale; the style, flat-statement realism; the surface emotion, absurdist: "Then I remembered: he was run over by a carriage." Abruptly, a surrealist image breaks in:

> The man sitting in the center of the bed looks very much like my father. He is weeping, tears coursing down his cheeks. One can see that he is upset about something. Looking at him I see that something is wrong. He is spewing like a fire hydrant with its locks knocked off. His yammer darts in and out of all the rooms. . . .

The portrait of the impossible dead father is of course ambiguous. The son is both concerned and dutiful, on one hand, and annoyed by the father's vulgarity and childishness, on the other ("yammer"), an ambivalence to be developed throughout the story. Two juxtaposed images show the contrast clearly, one showing the father as magical, hence vastly superior to the son, the other showing him as embarrassingly childlike, the very antithesis of "an aristocrat."

> My father throws his ball of knitting up in the air. The orange wool hangs there.
>
> .
>
> My father regards the tray of pink cupcakes. Then he jams his thumb into each cupcake, into the top. Cupcake by cupcake. A thick smile spreads over the face of each cupcake.

The story continues in alternating passages of parodic nineteenth-century gothic detective fiction (with modifications), surrealist fiction, and other styles. With the help of witnesses, the son traces the driver of the aristocrat's carriage, a man named Lars Bang; we learn that, just as he is ashamed of his father, the son feels ashamed of his own inadequacy by the aristocratic standard ("When I heard this name [Lars Bang], which in its sound and appearance is rude, vulgar, not unlike my own name, I was seized by repugnance. . . ."); and finally, in company with other listeners, the son learns from the carriage driver (an elegant man in comparison to the son) that the father's death was a result of his own foolishness—he was drunk and attacked the horses with a switch. Instead of winning justice for a murdered father, the son has learned—and caused others to learn—of his father's shame and guilt, thereby increasing his own. Yet perhaps this is wrong (reality is impenetrable). A beautiful young girl, who has sat silent and sullen through Bang's recitation, abruptly speaks up (using language slightly vulgar): " 'Bang is an absolute bloody liar,' she said." The story ends, as it must: "Etc." As in *The Dead Father*, the burden of sons goes on and on.

What is most striking about the story is the range of styles orchestrated for a single effect: gothic detective fiction, surrealism, old-style melodrama (as here):

> Why! . . . there's my father . . . sitting in the bed there! . . . and he's *weeping*! . . . as though his heart would burst! . . . Father! . . . how is this? . . . who has wounded you? . . . name the man! . . . why I'll . . . I'll . . . here, Father, take this handkerchief! . . . and this handkerchief! . . . and this handkerchief! . . . I'll run for a towel. . . .

Or again, absurdist verbal comedy:

> Then we shot up some mesquite bushes and some parts of a Ford pickup somebody'd left lying around. But no animals came to our party (it was noisy, I admit it). A long list of animals failed to arrive, no deer, quail, rabbit, seals, sea lions, condylarths. . . .

Et cetera. What holds it all together is the narrative voice, a comic-pathetic troubled mind.

All of these approaches to fiction—expressionist, surrealist, absurdist, irrealist—produce interesting work if the writer is any good, however shaky the philosophical base. When the writer creates something new, he can hardly help doing it at least by analogy to the familiar creative process, turning street sounds or electronic bleeps into "music" by analogy to the process by which Bach and those before him made music of notes, or creating an oral sculpture by a method analogous to that of the traditional sculptor or film-maker. At the "objective" end of Robert Louis Stevenson's continuum, the end that attracts the irrealists, the only human reality that remains is the selecting process of the artist. We get from the work his emotional set, the affirmation—even if he doesn't wish to make it—of his eye's relationship (and therefore his heart's) to things. The same goes for the super-realists. As Robbe-Grillet keeps pointing out, you cannot get down the reality of the refrigerator when no one is in the room; in other words, writers cannot suppress "the mental constructs through which they are peering." The whole question of the uncertainty principle is in a sense a red herring. We choose techniques as we choose words in English, either to say what we mean, as nearly as we can, or to find out what happens when we choose those techniques, those words. "I hate you," the child says to his father, watching shrewdly for reaction. "Marriage is a strange thing," says the lover, and glances at his love. So I propose in a piece of fiction that a certain man had three hundred sons, all red-heads, and I muse on what that makes me say next.

Let us turn to specifics. Out of the horde of technical matters that might be mentioned I will choose seven that seem to me basic: learning technique by imitation, development and control of vocabulary, sentence handling, poetic rhythm, point of view, delay, and style. On all these matters, my discussion is meant to be suggestive, not exhaustive.

Imitation

For centuries, one of the standard ways of learning techniques has been imitation, as when, in the eighteenth century, the student took some classical model—for example, the Pindaric hymn or the Horatian ode—and wrote, in Greek, Latin, or English, an original work in imitation of that model. The approach is still instructive. Two kinds of imitation seem especially worthwhile: careful use of an old, generally unfamiliar form for the presentation and analysis of modern subject matter, and the more direct, even line-by-line imitation that enables the writer to learn "from inside" the secrets of some great writer's style.

Though human experience is universal in many ways, attitudes change from age to age, and one way of coming to understand our ideas and emotions is to study them through the spectacles of some earlier form or set of aesthetic premises. For a number of reasons, we cannot quite share the Romantic experience of nature. For one thing, nature itself has changed. Whereas the Romantic artist might make a painting he calls "Tree and Stream" or "View of Mont-Sainte-Victoire, Late Afternoon," the painter today, whether from disillusionment or from a curious but authentic attachment to the world he knows, may make a painting he calls "Pontiac with Treetrunk" or "Chevy in Green Fields." In the same way, the writer may copy some old idea—the dream vision, the imaginary voyage, the hymn to the state, the saint's legend, or the framed narrative—and may translate the form to suit modern experience. So in *Jason and Medeia* I copied the *Argonautica* of Apollonios Rhodios (with some additions from Euripides and others), asking myself at every turn what the characters and events might mean to a modern sensibility—asking, that is, how much of the original would still hold, how much we are forced to alter and why, whose reading of experience is more accurate (that of Apollonios or our own), and how much experience itself has changed. So Donald Barthelme plays off the medieval tradition of the allegorical mountain (mainly off Chaucer's *The House of Fame*) in "The Glass Mountain," Stanley Elkin imitates *The Canterbury Tales* in *The Dick Gibson Show*, John Barth imitates Scheherazade in *Chimera*, and James Joyce in a sense imitates the *Odyssey*. Working closely with some earlier work, scrutinizing the older writer's way of doing things, the modern writer gets an angle on his material. He learns how the speech of modern heroes must differ from that of old-fashioned heroes (he learns the advantages and drawbacks of decadence), learns why the innocent Homeric simile has given way to modern, more ironic simile, learns why traditional allegory has become for us an all but dead option except in comic works.

The imitations I've mentioned—Barthelme, and so on—are all fairly sophisticated; that is, far removed from the base of imitation. Much closer following of the model can achieve equally interesting—and new—results. Many of Poe's stories are imitations or parodic comments. His "Imp of the Perverse," for instance, imitates the style of Washington Irving and attacks the philistinism and anti-intellectualism of Irving's "Legend of Sleepy Hollow." Though we sometimes associate parody with college humor magazines or such popular organs as *Mad* magazine and the *National Lampoon*, the use of parodic technique, both comic and serious, has proved a rich vein for contemporary writers. (It has been a mainstay of poets for centuries.) The parodist may use only the general style of his model, as Robert Coover in "A Pedestrian Accident" (from *Pricksongs and Descants*) uses slapstick film-comedy and vaudeville routines for a grim new purpose, or he may follow his model almost line for line, merely changing details of action, character, and setting. Whether or not the result is art will depend on the writer's wit. Either way, the exercise will produce a clearer knowledge of how the writer achieved his effects.

Vocabulary

A huge vocabulary is not always an advantage. Simple language, for some kinds of fiction at least, can be more effective than complex language, which can lead to stiltedness or suggest dishonesty or faulty education. One of the surest signs of limited taste or intellectual mediocrity—though sometimes it signals only shyness and insecurity—is continual use of the same polysyllabic or foreign words everyone else uses, fashionable words like "serendipity," or "ubiquitous"; "*genre*," "*milieu*," and "*ambiance*" when emphasized as French; worn-out German words or phrases like "*Weltanschauung*," "*Gestalt*," or "*Sturm und Drang*"; or jargon words like "fictional strategy." And the writer who uses his own fancy language, not just that which is in style, can be equally offensive. If we sense that, though working as a realist, he writes mainly for elegant verbal effect, choosing his characters for the cleverness of their chatter or even violating character out of deference to his ear, using "calculate" for "think" or giving all his characters the right to say "dastardly," "*comme il faut*," or "my man," we sense mannerism and frigidity and at once back off. This rule, like all rules, must be applied with good sense. Dostoevsky chooses characters for the kinds of things they'll talk about. And a noticeably ornate vocabulary can be a splendid thing if well used. For the writer who handles difficult or obscure words well, giving the appearance of introducing them smoothly and effortlessly, violating neither the authorial tone nor fidelity to character, ornate vocabulary can extend the writer's range of tone and give textural richness, to say nothing of increased precision. For symbolists and allegorists like Hawthorne and Melville, ornate vocabulary may be an absolute requisite. In effective writing—normally—the writer slips in symbols and allegorical emblems with the cunning of a flim-flam man gulling his country victim. The symbol that stands out too sharply from its matrix may distract the reader's eye from the fictional dream, with the unpleasing effect of making the writer seem frigid and his story disingenuous, more sermon than honest presentation of imagined events—a work, in short, in which the reader feels manipulated, pushed toward some opinion or view of the world not inherent in the fictional materials but imposed from above.

"Normally," I've said. In a certain kind of fiction clunky symbolism, or the appearance of wooden allegory, can be a source of delight, and a vocabulary of extremely odd words like "furfuraceous," "venditate," or "ignivomous," words that function like baubles or textural blisters, calling attention to the story's artificiality, can give interest. For comic effect, one can do anything that's funny. And to those who appreciate it, part of the appeal of Chaucer's *Man of Law's Tale* is its stiffness, its rigidity of idea and emotion. Cunstance never seems to us a real woman. She has the hard angles of a primitive carving or a figure in stained glass; her story starts and stops with the jerks and creaks of old machinery, and we enjoy it precisely because of what nowadays we would call its irreality—its base in an outmoded set of literary conventions. The same is true of Chaucer's *Second Nun's Tale* and of any number of modern parodic works both serious and comic. By making one's symbolism unusually obvious, as in the best moments of Barth's *Giles Goat-Boy*, one can sometimes get a pleasing effect of artifice without in fact sacrificing the symbolic load. We smile at the clunkiness of the allegory but at the same time follow the allegory out, much as in puppet shows or Noh plays we enjoy both the emphasis on technique and its import.

Normally, however, the symbolist or allegorist works more subtly. In "Bartleby the Scrivener," Melville uses, as he often does, a narrator capable of orbicular language because it allows him to introduce double meanings—allegorizing puns—without disturbing the surface of the story. On its most obvious level, the story is of a compassionate lawyer rendered helpless by the dilemma of both keeping up his work in the ordinary business world and dealing humanely with what turns out to be the cosmic despair, in fact madness, of his copyist Bartleby. On a deeper level, the lawyer is a kind of Jehovah figure, Bartleby a pathetic and ineffective Christ who binds Jehovah to a new idea of justice. The lawyer-narrator's formal, even ponderous diction allows Melville to treat the surface story with full respect for the dignity of his characters and their pathetic situation but at the same time to work in signals of the deeper meaning. Melville writes:

> This view [the white wall the narrator sees through one of his windows] might have been considered rather tame than otherwise deficient in what landscape painters call "life." But, if so, the view from the other end of my chambers offered, at least, a contrast, if nothing more. In

that direction, my windows commanded an unobstructed view of a lofty brick wall, blackened by age and everlasting shade. . . .

At first glance, these sentences are merely descriptive of the narrator's suite of offices, with a white wall at one window, a brick wall at another. But the narrator's elevated diction allows in language that hints at the deeper meaning that Bartleby will call to his attention: His comfortable "upstairs" chambers are surrounded by death. This kind of thing runs all through the story, establishing its full symbolic meaning.

I have spoken so far only of ornate vocabulary. A common problem among beginning writers is that even their vocabulary of ordinary words is limited to a degree almost crippling. Ordinary words, like rare words, give textural interest. The good writer is likely to know and use—or find out and use—the words for common architectural features, like "lintel," "newel post," "corbelling," "abutment," and the concrete or stone "hems" alongside the steps leading up into churches or public buildings; the names of carpenters' or plumbers' tools, artists' materials, or whatever furniture, implements, or processes his characters work with; and the names of common household items, including those we do not usually hear named, often as we use them, such as "pinch-clippers" (for cutting fingernails). The writer, if it suits him, should also know and occasionally use brand names, since they help to characterize. The people who drive Toyotas are not the same people who drive BMW's, and people who brush with Crest are different from those who use Pepsodent or, on the other hand, one of the health-food brands made of eggplant. (In super-realist fiction, brand names are more important than the characters they describe.) Above all, the writer should stretch his vocabulary of ordinary words and idioms— words and idioms he sees all the time and knows how to use but never uses. I mean here not language that smells of the lamp but relatively common verbs, nouns, and adjectives—"galumph" and "amble," "quagmire," "scoop" (n.), "pustule," "hippodrome," "distraught," "recalcitrant," "remiss." The casual way to build vocabulary is to pay attention to language as one reads. The serious-minded way is to read through a dictionary, making lists of all the common words one happens never to use. And of course the really serious-minded way is to study languages— learn Greek, Latin, and one or two modern languages. Among writers of the first rank one can name very few who were not or are not fluent in at least two. Tolstoy, who spoke Russian, French, and English easily, and other languages and dialects with more difficulty, studied Greek in his forties.

The immediate risk for the writer who works hard at developing vocabulary is that his style may become texturally over-rich, distracting from the fictional dream. But practice teaches balance. Limited vocabulary, like short legs on a pole-vaulter, builds in a natural barrier to progress beyond a certain point.

The Sentence

After the individual word, the writer's most basic unit of expression is the sentence, the primary vehicle of all rhetorical devices. One of the things that should go into the writer's notebook is a set of experiments with the sentence. A convenient and challenging place to begin is with the long sentence, one that runs to at least two pages. (For a *tour-de-force* example see Donald Barthelme's piece of short fiction "Sentence"—in fact not a long, long sentence but a fragment.) Long sentences, one soon learns—and I mean not fake long sentences, wherein commas, semicolons, and colons could be changed into periods with no loss of emotional power or intellectual coherence, but *real* sentences—can be of many kinds, each with its own unique effects. The sentence may be propelled by some driving, hysterical emotion, like William Faulkner's long sentence in the occasionally included introduction to *The Sound and the Fury*, in which the town librarian finds Caddy's picture in a magazine, closes the library, and rushes with the picture, her wits flying and her heart wildly pounding, to Jason's store; or the sentence may be kept aloft—that is, held back from the relief of a final close, a full stop for breath, in other words, a period—by some neurotic sense of hesitation in the character whose troubled mental processes the sentence is designed to reflect—some intelligent middle-aged housewife, for example, who has read about women's liberation in her magazines and feels an increasingly anxious inclination, hedged in by doubts and on-the-other-hands, to take a nightschool course—one in flower-arranging, or ceramics, or self-awareness—perhaps telling her domineering mother and husband what she's doing and then again perhaps not—though money will be a problem if she takes the course secretly: She has only her household and grocery allowance— and there are always the children, though Mark (let us call him) might possibly be talked into staying after school Thursday nights to play basketball, and Daniel, on the other hand . . . but would Daniel even miss her if she went out, in fact?—glued every night to the TV in his room, smoking (if that's what the smell is) pot?—but it would be risky, no doubt of it; if they found her out—Harold and her mother—there would be scenes, tiresome dramas; better to find some more foolproof plan . . . or the sentence may be kept going by the complexity of its thought, or by the ornateness of its imagery, or by the "sheer plod" of the drudge it illustrates, or by some other cause, or motor, before at last it quits.

Short sentences give other effects. Also sentence fragments. They can be trenchant, punchy. They can suggest weariness. They can increase the drabness of a drab scene. Used for an unworthy reason, as here, they can be boring.

Between these extremes, the endless sentence and the very short sentence, lies a world of variation, a world every writer must eventually explore.

Poetic Rhythm

1. Prose, like poetry, is built of rhythms and rhythmic variations.

2. Like poetry, prose has rhythms and rhythmic variations.

3. Rhythm and variation are as basic to prose as to poetry.

4. All prose must force rhythms, just like verse.*

Compare the above. Reading at the natural speed we use for prose, faster than the natural speed of verse or prose poetry, we find that item 2 is slower, more plodding, than item 1; and item

---

* Metrical analysis markings are always approximations, both when we're dealing with prose and when we deal with verse. Other good readers— or I myself on another day—might legitimately read the lines I've marked in other ways, though some readings are sure to be less convincing than others. I use the symbols for metrical analysis, here and in the rest of this discussion, as follows: ′ = stressed syllable; ` = lightly stressed syllable (or sometimes, in metrical verse, beat in the absence of stress); ‿ = unstressed syllable; ¯ = unstressed but long or slow syllable; ↥ = unstressed syllable slightly oonched (by rhyme or some other force) toward stress; ‖ = pause or caesura; ⌢ = hovering stress (also $\overset{2}{\frown{/\!/}}$), used in situations where we might read two juxtaposed syllables as either trochaic or iambic, but so similar in stress that they seem to divide the emphasis of beat between them, as in Robert Frost's

Whose woods these are I think I know

or—

Whose woods these are I think I know.

When in verse three or more stresses (either in juxtaposition or with one or more interposed unstressed syllables) seem to share a single beat, the phrase mark and stress number may be useful: $\overset{3}{\frown{/\!/\!/}}$. (In rhythmically tricky metrical verse, think of the beat as the drum's basic rhythm, and the variations as the jazz soloist's syncopated ride.) The

3, because of the fairly regular occurrence of stressed syllables and the number of unstressed syllables between them, runs along more lightly than either 1 or 2 and much more lightly than item 4, where the juxtaposed stresses slow the sentence to a trudge.

---

reason for these complications, hovering stress and phrase, is that in metrical English verse a foot can normally contain no more than one stressed and two unstressed syllables, though occasionally—especially in nursery rhymes and some very old folk poetry—one or more extra unstressed syllables may be slipped in—the extra syllables Gerard Manley Hopkins called "riders." By the system I am using, the only possible patterns for the English foot, discounting riders and other syncopations, are iambic ($\smile$ $/$), trochaic ($/$ $\smile$), dactylic ($/$ $\smile$ $\smile$), anapestic ($\smile$ $\smile$ $/$), and amphibrachic ($\smile$ $/$ $\smile$). In verse, the number of *feet* in the line gives the line's meter. For instance, the Frost line just quoted

$$\text{Whose woóds} \mid \text{these áre} \mid \text{I thínk} \mid \text{I knów}$$

has four beats (as marked). The basic measures are monometer, dimeter, trimeter, tetrameter, pentamenter, hexameter, and heptameter. Beyond this length the line tends to break into separate parts, as octameter, for instance, tends to read as two joined tetrameters. Only on rare occasions, as in some of the writings of William Gass, and in some of my own work, does prose rhythm contain meter—usually hidden, since the metrically equal lines are run together, though they may give some such signal of their presence as obvious or subtle rhyme.

A knowledge of verse scansion is no idle talent for the prose writer. Really good prose differs in only one way from good contemporary verse —by which one means, mainly, free verse (unrhymed and metrically irregular). Verse slows the reader by means of line breaks; prose does not. Note that these lines, by poet and fiction writer Joyce Carol Oates, could be set either as prose or as verse:

The car plunges westward into the bluing dusk of New York State.
There is no end to it: the snakes that writhe in the headlights,
the scarves of snow, the veins, vines, tendrils,
the sky a crazy broken blue
like crockery.

Some contemporary free verse, like that of Galway Kinnell, has more compression than prose can bear; no one denies the power of Kinnell's best verse, but as Whitman proves, compression of that sort is not an absolute requirement.

In good prose, rhythm never stumbles, slips into accidental doggerel, or works against the meaning of the sentence. Consider the following sentence permutations. (For my convenience, assume that the ice has been established by context and may be omitted when we like.)

1. The pig thrashed and squealed, then lay helpless on the ice, panting and trembling.

2. After thrashing and squealing, the pig lay helpless, panting and trembling.

3. Thrashing and squealing, then panting, trembling, the pig lay helpless on the ice.

4. The pig thrashed and squealed, then, panting, trembling, lay helpless.

Rhythmically, item 1 seems not entirely satisfactory. The final phrase, "panting and trembling," comes as a kind of afterthought—we don't feel propelled into it by all that has gone before—and its faint echo of the earlier rhythm, "thrashed and squealed," feels slightly awkward. Item 2 is worse: The echo of "thrashing and squealing" is now much too obvious, giving the sentence an offensive clunky symmetry. Item 3 is better. The echoing phrases have been brought together in the same part of the sentence, allowing the close of the sentence to smooth out and run free; and by dropping the word "and" from the phrase "panting and trembling," the rhythm of this segment is slowed down ("panting, trembling") and the echo is to some extent suppressed. And 4 is better yet. Slowed by the phrase "panting, trembling," the sentence winds down, like the pig, in the word "helpless." Sound now echoes sense.

By keeping out a careful ear for rhythm, the writer can control the emotion of his sentences with considerable subtlety. In my novel *Grendel,* I wanted to establish the emotion and character of the central-character monster in his first utterance. After some brooding and fiddling, I wrote:

The old ram stands looking down over rockslides, stupidly triumphant.

Part of the effect, if the sentence works, is of course the choice of words. It would be different if I'd written, "The old cow sits . . ." But part of it is the handling of stresses. The opening juxtaposed stresses, intensified by near rhyme, give appropriate harshness; the alliteration of an essentially nasty sound ("*st*ands," "*st*upidly") maintains this quality; and the rhythmic hesitation of the long syllable at the end of the first phrase

rockslides

followed by the tumble into difficult-to-manage supernumerary unstressed syllables

stupidly triumphant

gives a suggestion—I hope—of the monster's clumsiness of thought and gait. (We scan the words, I think, as

stupidly tri umphant

rather than as dactylic and amphibrachic. Thus "tri" functions —or would in metrical verse—as a rider, and, given our habits of expectation in strongly rhythmic prose as in verse, the syllables fall clumsily.)

The good writer works out his rhythms by ear; he usually has no need of the paraphernalia I've invoked here for purposes of discussion. Yet occasionally it proves helpful to scan a line with metrical analysis marks, as an aid to determining where some new, strong beat should be inserted, or some pair of unstressed syllables suppressed or added. Turning sentences around, trying various combinations of the fundamental elements, will prove invaluable in the end, not just because it leads to better sentences but also because over the years it teaches certain basic ways of fixing rhythm that will work again on other, superficially quite dissimilar sentences. I don't know, myself—and I suspect most writers would say the same—what it is that I do, what formulas I use for switching bad sentences around to make better ones; but I do it all the time, less laboriously every year, trying to creep up on the best ways of getting things said. One thing that may be helpful to notice is the kinds of changes that push unstressed syllables up to stress. Take the first phrase of the nursery rhyme "Taffy Was a Welshman." Rhythmically the poem can legitimately be viewed in two ways, either as regular metrical verse or as "old native meter," derivative from the Old English alliterative line. In the former case the line has six beats, in the latter only four. I will treat the line here as old native meter. Watch the permutations pushing unstressed syllables to stress, or, as Hopkins would say, "springing" the verse.

Taffy was a Welshman, Taffy was a thief.

1. Taffy was a damn fool,

2. Taffy shot a damn fool,

3. Bill Jones shot a damn fool,

4. Bill Jones shot two damn fools,

Notice the difference of energy in the various rhythmic permutations, though behind all the jazzing the (imaginary) drumbeat is the same.

Point of View

What has already been said on the subject of point of view need not be repeated here. In contemporary writing one may do anything one pleases with point of view, as long as it works. As long as the flavor of the writing is at once contemporary (as a John Salt painting or a George Segal sculpture simply could not come from any other time), one need not send signals to the reader that one may do peculiar things—sudden shifts of any kind. That is part of the built-in expectation and pleasure of "contemporary" or at-once-recognizably-innovative art. But in every age, including our own, some literature—often the best, since as a rule one cannot simultaneously invent wildly and think deeply —some literature uses traditional methods, and here a certain correctness is beyond dismissal. Some discussion of point of view is therefore necessary.

It is often said, mainly by non-writers, that the first-person point of view (the "I" point of view, as in "then I saw the jug") is the most natural. This is doubtful. The third-person point of view ("Then she saw the jug") is more common in both folk and sophisticated narrative. No fairy tales are told in the first person; also no jokes. First person allows the writer to write as he talks, and this may be an advantage for intelligent people who have interesting speech patterns and come from a culture with a highly developed oral tradition, such as American blacks, Jews, and southern or down-east Yankee yarn-spinners; but first person does not force the writer to recognize that written speech has to make up for the loss of facial expression, gesture, and the like, and the usual result is not good writing but only writing less noticeably bad.

Once first-person narrative has been mastered—by some standard of mastery—the writer is encouraged to write in the third person subjective, a point of view in which all the "I"s are changed to "he"s or "she"s and emphasis is placed on the character's thoughts, so that "Then she saw the jug" becomes, "Was that a *jug* she saw?" or "A jug! she thought." This point of view (style, in a sense) goes for deep consciousness, in the hope that the thoughts and feelings of the character will become the immediate (unmediated) thoughts and feelings of the reader. The effect is something like:

> Was that a *jug* she saw? No, she must not touch that honey jug! Old Doc China had chortled, "You lose ninety pounds, Lulu Bogg, or you're a goner. Like your ma before you. You'll sit up in bed some one of these mornings and you'll turn white with the effort of it, and *click*." Doc had snapped his fingers, brown, bony fingers that wouldn't go fat if you fed 'em on goose fat and white bread for a month.

The third-person-subjective point of view has its uses, but it also has severe limits, so that something is wrong when it becomes the dominant point of view in fiction, as it has been for years in the United States. In addition to defects mentioned already (Chapter 3), it locks the reader inside the character's mind (even more so than Henry James' "center of consciousness," where we have an interpreting narrator), however limited that mind may be, so that when the character's judgments are mistaken or inadequate, the reader's more correct judgments must come from a cool withdrawal. When the fiction is judgmental, and for some reason much third-person-subjective fiction is, the writer commits himself to nothing except by irony; he merely exposes the stupidities of mankind; and except insofar as he misses the point, the reader stands apart from the action of the story, watching it critically, like a grumpy old man at a party. One can of course get the same misanthropic effect by means of other techniques; for instance, by use of the crabby omniscient narrator of Katherine Anne Porter's fiction or the darkly ironic voice sometimes favored by Melville, as in *The Confidence Man*. And on the other hand it is of course possible for a writer using the third-person-subjective point of view to enjoy and admire his characters; to write, that is, about someone he considers at least in some measure a hero. But even when the fiction is benevolent, the third-person-subjective point of view can achieve little grandeur. It thrives on intimacy and something like gossip. It peeks through a keyhole, never walks through an open field.

An even less grand point of view is third person *objective*, identical to third person subjective except that the narrator not only never comments himself but also refrains from entering any character's mind. The result is an ice-cold camera's-eye recording. We see events, hear dialogue, observe the setting, and make guesses about what the characters are thinking. This point of view can work brilliantly in fairly short fiction. Its limits are obvious.

The noblest writers, like Isak Dinesen and Leo Tolstoy, rise above the pettiness and unseemly familiarity of third person subjective, and avoid the savage sparsity of third person objective, by means of the authorial-omniscient point of view. In the authorial omniscient, the writer speaks as, in effect, God. He sees into all his characters' hearts and minds, presents all positions with justice and detachment, occasionally dips into the third person subjective to give the reader an immediate sense of why the character feels as he does, but reserves to himself the right to judge (a right he uses sparingly). Usually he judges events, touching on morality only by implication. When he intrudes with moral heavy-handedness, as Tolstoy does in *Resurrection*, the effect is likely to be disaster. In the authorial-omniscient point of view the reader escapes the claustrophobia he may feel when boxed into a limited opinion; he sees and celebrates, shrugs off, or deplores a variety of opinions; and he sails along securely, confident that he will not be tricked or betrayed by the wise and thoughtful narrator. The cards are on the table.

What for a time demoted the authorial-omniscient point of view—ruler of the field for centuries—was widespread doubt, at least among intellectuals, about the existence of God, and increasing fascination with Pilate's tiresome question "What is Truth?" Charles Dickens, Joseph Conrad, Henry James, Stephen Crane, and many others invented valuable alternatives to the omniscient voice—among others, the story told through various points of view, filtered through perhaps unreliable narrators like Conrad's Marlow, or reported by some poetic or real voice, even the imagined voice of the community. Now that nervous theological and metaphysical questions have lost their wide appeal, writers like Donald Barthelme, Joyce Carol Oates, or William Gass feel free to use the omniscient point of view whenever they like, untroubled by God's existence or nonexistence and its furthermores. The authorial-omniscient narrator is, for them, as much a fiction (or a literary tradition without desperate implications) as anything else they may use in their writing, such as the old palomino horse with spavins, or the wired-up chair in some kitchen. Cutting through the muck, they simply say—in the traditional voice of the omniscient narrator—what is fictionally true. They play God as they might play King Claudius, by putting on a cape.

One of the problems the beginner may encounter in using the authorial-omniscient point of view is that of establishing it in the first place and, throughout his story, moving smoothly into the minds of his characters. To establish this point of view when his narrative opens, the writer must dip fairly soon into various minds, setting up the rules; that is, establishing the expectation that, when he likes, he will move from consciousness to consciousness. The shift to third person subjective requires a skillful handling of psychic distance. (On psychic distance, see p. 111.)

Another available point of view is the so-called "essayist omniscient." The easiest way to describe it is by contrast with the authorial omniscient. The language of the authorial-omniscient voice is traditional and neutral: The author speaks with dignity and proper grammar, saying what any calm, dignified, and reasonable person would say. "Happy families are all alike." Or: "During the first quarter of the last century, seaside resorts became the fashion, even in those countries of Northern Europe within the minds of whose people the sea had hitherto held the role of the Devil, the cold and voracious hereditary foe of humanity." Every authorial-omniscient voice sounds much like every other. The essayist-omniscient voice, though it has nearly the same divine authority, is more personal. Though we do not know the name and occupation of the speaker, we sense at once that the voice is old or young, male or female, black (as in Charles Johnson's *Faith and the Good Thing*) or white. Whereas the writer who has chosen the authorial-omniscient technique needs only to imitate, say, Tolstoy, the writer using the essayist-omniscient voice must first invent a character with particular habits of thought and particular speech patterns. Except by their concerns and subject matter, one cannot tell Tolstoy from Dinesen. Neither is free to be sly or bitchy; the voice simply states facts and makes seemingly impartial judgments. Jane Austen, on the other hand, can say anything she pleases, as long as it's interesting and suitable to the personal voice established. Until recently most writers who used the essayist voice developed some one distinctive voice and used it book after book (Edgar Allan Poe, Mark Twain, William Faulkner). Contemporary writers tend to play more with ventriloquism, so that sometimes one book by a given writer sounds very little like another by the same writer.

Delay

All good fiction contains suspense, different kinds of suspense in different kinds of fiction. Take the simplest kind first.

Anyone can write "A shot rang out" or "There lay the body of Mrs. Uldridge." What is harder to write is the moment leading up to such a climax. When the writing is successful, the reader senses that the climax is coming and feels a strong urge to skip to it directly, but cannot quite tear himself from the paragraph he's on. Ideally, every element in the lead-in passage should be a relevant distraction that heightens the reader's anticipation and at the same time holds, itself, such interest—through richness of literal or metaphoric language, through startling accuracy of perception, or through the deepening thematic and emotional effect of significant earlier moments recalled—that the reader is reluctant to dash on.

Even in the work of some of our better pop novelists, too easy solutions to this problem are common. One is the author's first- or third-person entry into the suspense-filled thoughts of a character, in the hope that the character's suspense will rub off on the reader. Another, more general, is irrelevant distraction: "As I walked toward the Parker place, there was a mockingbird singing. Upstairs, it sounded like—somewhere behind the shutters—though I knew there couldn't be a mockingbird inside. I remembered—moving without a sound toward the gate —how Old Bass used to tell me about mockingbirds. 'Samuel,' he'd say . . ." Irrelevant distraction, even if it works, in a feeble way, makes the reader feel manipulated. True, texture can help disguise the fault (the name Old Bass here, the mockingbird); and true, the line between irrelevant distraction and relevant distraction may be a fine one. The distracting detail of thought about the mockingbird, in the lines above, is not irrelevant if it recalls earlier passages in the fiction, associations that enrich the suspenseful moment. Old Bass may have died mysteriously, or may have believed that the song of a mockingbird presages dark events.

We are all familiar with those obligatory moments in suspenseful movies when the lady is about to open the dangerous door. She stops to listen, eyebrows lifted, and if the movie's a good one the sound that has troubled her is one we've heard before (though she, perhaps, has not), a sound we too were troubled by at first, until we learned that it was only the tin cup hanging on the pump-spout, banging in the wind. Or the distracting sound may recall a scene that contrasts with this one; for example, a scene in which little Leander, now ominously vanished, played happily with the hired man's cat, offering it a drink. The lady moves forward again, her fear allayed, and reaches cautiously toward the door we don't want her to open. Another sound! She pauses, her expression partly fear, partly irritation—irritation at her own timidity, perhaps, but the expression is one into which we're free to project our own irritation. (Suspenseful delay is enjoyable, but even when distractions enrich the meaning of the climax about to come, we are not such fools as to miss the fact that we're being led, a little like donkeys. If the reader is not to waken from the fictional dream, it can be useful to anticipate the reader's feeling and channel it back into the story.)

Another kind of delay may be achieved by stylistic juxtaposition. Early in "Views of My Father Weeping," Donald Barthelme introduces surrealist elements—in this case images from outside the flow of time—into a narrative that has so far been profluent, or forward-moving. We are puzzled for a moment, wondering whence came the strange image of the dead father weeping on the bed, then the image of his throwing the ball of yarn, then that of his mashing the cupcakes. Before we can figure out the answer, we are thrown back into profluence, only to be brought up short again, a page or two later, by more surrealism. The effect, though more subtle and intellectual, is a little like that in a thriller novel when the author leaves one character and sequence of events for another not immediately relevant to the first but sure to intersect with it eventually. So, for instance, the writer may begin with a likable American family of tourists arriving in Hong Kong, then switch to a group of dangerous international plotters. Mentally casting forward, the reader expects trouble for the tourists and feels the beginning twinges of suspense. Here, as in Barthelme, the suspense comes partly from our not knowing for sure where we are or how to anticipate the future.

In serious fiction, the highest kind of suspense involves the Sartrian anguish of choice; that is, our suspenseful concern is not just with what will happen but with the moral implications of action. Given two possible choices, each based on some approvable goal, we worry, as we read, over which choice the character will make and, given the nature of reality, what the results will be.

In some recent fiction, notably that of Samuel Beckett and, often, Donald Barthelme, the writer makes ironic use of the fictional convention of delay, encouraging the reader to cast forward to some possible outcome and then refusing to make any progress toward that end. In *Waiting for Godot* we are told that the two tramps have come to this barren place to wait for Godot, whoever that may be. The tramps talk and go through circular motions—routines leading nowhere—and time passes, in the sense that things happen (though not sequentially): The one remaining leaf falls from its branch on the nearly barren tree; but Godot does not arrive. Our conventional expectation helps Beckett make his point on stasis. In Beckett's play *Happy Days* we get much the same thing. The pile of refuse in which one of the two characters is buried gets deeper act by act—by the third it is up to her neck; but despite this proof that time is passing, the characters learn nothing, make no progress. In Barthelme, the end may be achieved but, if so, proves to be some idiotic joke, as at the end of "The Glass Mountain" or *The Dead Father*—a joke that makes nonsense of the quest. In these works delay becomes an end in itself—the value, if any, is in the journey, not the arrival—and the anguish of choice proves a fool's delusion, since no choice brings satisfaction. The art of such fiction lies in keeping the reader going, though the writer knows from the beginning that there's no place to go. The moral value of such writing is obviously dubious, though it can be argued—by emphasizing the moral seriousness of the writer as he presents his suspect opinions; by pointing out, if possible, the measure of authentic compassion we can feel for the characters (not just pity or ironic detachment); or by maintaining that, in laughing, we at once accept and reject the conceit. We accept, much as we do when we hear sick jokes, in that we see how the writer might say such an outrageous thing; we reject in that, in the act of laughing, we deny that human beings are the helpless clown-creatures the author has represented, and we suspect, rightly or wrongly, that the author secretly agrees with us—otherwise why make the characters so clownlike? The fact that Samuel Beckett is in earnest, or says he is, may surprise us but does not change our response. To the writer who wishes to emulate Beckett or Barthelme, the only possible advice is this: Make sure your routines are as interesting as your model's.

Style

About style, the less said the better. Nothing leads to fraudulence more swiftly than the conscious pursuit of stylistic uniqueness. But on the other hand nothing is more natural to the young and ambitious writer than that he try to find a voice and territory of his own, proving himself different from all other writers. Such a young writer is likely to take advice from no one, and though that fact may exasperate his writing teacher, the wise teacher knows it's an excellent sign, and gives the young writer his head, objecting to and criticizing stylistic absurdities only enough to keep the student honest.

A few observations may be made to the young stylist that may prove useful. First, most fictional styles are traditional—think, for example, of the customary style of the tale, the yarn, the third-person-omniscient realistic piece of fiction. Many writers simply master one such style and make use of it all their lives, counting on their own unique experience and personality to make the style individual. They are right to do so, though their choice is not the only one available. Each writer's interests and personality must inevitably modify the style. Someone who writes brilliantly, with closely observed detail, about professional dishwashing or clerking in a grocery store, presenting his material in the normal style of third-person-subjective realistic fiction, must inevitably sound different from another writer who, working in the same basic style, writes of circus work or the life of professional torturers. Style often takes care of itself.

The same is true of the writer who masters not one conventional style but many, either writing each story in a style different from the style he used last time or mixing styles within a given story in a way that seems to him intuitively satisfying and somehow justifiable in terms of the story as a whole.

But there will always be those writers, rightly enough, who insist on creating some new style of their own, as Joyce did, or Faulkner, or William Gass. All that can be said to such writers is: Go to it. The risks are obvious: that the style will attract too much attention to itself; that the style may seem mannered; and that instead of freeing the writer to express himself it may limit the number and kinds of things he can say. (We see such limitations in Hemingway's early experiments with the third-person-objective point of view done with tough-guy simplicity.) Good criticism will help, if the writer can get it, and will take it. Failing that, time is likely to soften the style's excesses.

7

Plotting

When designing a profluent plot, we've said, the writer works in one of three ways, sometimes two or more at once: He borrows some traditional story or action drawn form life; he works backward from his climax; or he works forward from an initial situation. Without repetition of what has been said already, this chapter will examine all three of these methods as they apply to plotting short fiction, the novella, and the novel, and also examine ways of plotting other kinds of fiction, including the kind we call "plotless." The discussion cannot hope to be exhaustive, but it should give the beginner some practical guidance on the hardest job a writer ever does.

Though causal sequence gives the best (most obvious) kind of profluence, it is not the only possible means to that necessary end. A story or novel may develop argumentatively, leading the reader point by point to some conclusion. In this case events occur not to justify later events but to dramatize logical positions; thus event *a* does not cause event *b* but stands in some logical relation to it. So, for example, the writer might impose onto the twelve labors of Hercules—or some action from real life, or some fictional action—some logical sequence that, like any other interesting argument, keeps us reading. By dramatized concrete situations the writer argues, say, "If *a* does not work, try *b*; if *b* does not work, try *c*"—and so on through twelve possible modes of action or value possibilities. More specifically, the writer might show his central character trying to cope by charitable behavior, then, after failing, trying to cope by selfish behavior, and, failing again, trying to cope by a mixture of charity and selfish cunning, and so on until all options seem exhausted. Such a story or novel might be interesting, even brilliant, but it can never achieve the power of an energeic action because the control of action is intellectual, it does not rise out of the essence of things: It discusses reality the way a lecturer does (though perhaps more vividly), it does not reveal the modality of things. It does not capture process.

A related kind of profluence, which can also organize both made-up stories and traditional or real-life stories (found objects, so to speak), is the straight or modified picaresque plot. In traditional or pure form the picaresque narrative follows some character, often a clever rascal, from level to level through society, showing us the foibles and absurdities of each. The writer can make any substitutions he may please to pump new life into the old formula. Instead of the customary picaresque hero, he might use some monster from the fens—the monster Grendel, from *Beowulf*, for instance—and instead of the customary movement through the strata of society, he might choose a list of Great Ideas of Western Civilization (love, heroism, the artistic ideal, piety, and so forth) to which one by one he introduces his skeptical monster. This structuring of plot is likely to be more interesting or less depending on the extent to which the sequence raises questions involving the welfare of the character, each value, for instance, putting increasing pressure on the monster's skepticism. Insofar as the sequence of ideas provides some threat, the reader's involvement may be almost as great as it is in the well-built energeic plot, though here too the final energy is missing: the power of inexorable process.

Or again a plot may be constructed by symbolic juxtaposition. The epic *Beowulf*, discussed earlier, works in this way. All tales of quest, or nearly all, have this structure.

In the final analysis it seems unlikely that an essentially intellectual structure can have the same power and aesthetic validity, all other things being equal, as a structure that appeals simultaneously to our intellect and to subtler faculties, our deepest emotions (sympathy and empathy) and our intuition of reality's process. However that may be, an intellectual structure is easier to create than is a powerful energeic plot. With intellectual structures the writer always knows exactly where he stands and exactly where he's heading, though the reader may be baffled until he figures out the key. If the writer is very clever at fleshing out the skeleton, covering it with vivid details drawn from life or literature, the reader's initial bafflement, combined with his intuitive sense that the fiction has some order, may lead to the reader's at first overvaluing the work—and his later disappointment, when he figures it out. We sense at once some mysterious logic in Kafka's "A Country Doctor," and our first impulse is to attribute this mysterious coherence to some ingenious penetration of the nature of things. But once we learn that the story is tightly allegorical, as neat as mathematics or a sermon on the seven deadly sins, we may begin to find it thin and too obviously contrived. All this may be vain argument; certainly it does not deny Dante his status as the greatest of medieval poets. But in an age fond of intellectual structures, it is a thought worth considering that those writers who move us more profoundly than all others—Homer, Shakespeare, and Tolstoy, for example—differ not in degree but in kind from those masters whose structures are intellectual, not energeic— writers like Dante, Spenser, and Swift.

The question, to pose it one last way, is this: Can an argument manipulated from the start by the writer have the same emotional and intellectual power as an argument to which the writer is forced by his intuition of how life works? Comparisons are odious but instructive: Can a *Gulliver's Travels*, however brilliantly constructed, ever touch the hem of the garment of a play like *King Lear*? Or: Why is the *Aeneid* so markedly inferior to the *Iliad*?

From all we have said about plotting in general it should be evident that even in those "modern" plots in which events happen by laws not immediately visible—as when, for instance, the tattooed man in the circus reveals in the course of a whimsical conversation that he has on his chest a tattoo of the little girl now looking at him, a child he has never before seen, or as when, in Isak Dinesen, a decorous old nun turns abruptly into a monkey—there must be some rational or poetically persuasive basis. We can enjoy a story that has some secret logic we sense but cannot immediately guess; but if we begin to suspect that the basis of profluence is nothing but mad whimsey, we begin to be distracted from the fictional dream by our questions, doubts, and puzzlement, our feeling that the story is getting nowhere. The "mad" story—surrealist, expressionist, or whatever—must be as carefully plotted as the story with causally related actions.

One can plot such fiction in a variety of ways. The most common is the technique of setting up basic philosophical oppositions and then disguising them, translating ideas into appropriate characters and generating events by the method of the old-fashioned allegorist, each event expressing in mysterious but concrete terms the active relationship between the central ideas. Thus, for example, wishing to talk about materialism and spirituality, one might choose as allegorical "central characters" a fat banker and a pigeon; and wishing to say that body cannot live without soul or soul without body, we might set up a situation in which an elderly pigeon keeps up its strength by living off the crumbs that fall from the Oreo cookies the banker eats between cigars, and the banker is kept from dying of cigar-smoke asphyxiation by the necessity of from time to time opening the window to let the pigeon in and out. For contrast we might set up in the office next door an identical fat banker who does not have a pigeon, and an identical pigeon who has nothing for sustenance but rain. All of the images, needless to say (starting with the banker and the pigeon), are chosen both for their emblematic significance and for their inherent interest. (By an "emblem" I mean an image that has one signification. The banker means materialism and only materialism. By a "symbol" I mean an image that may mean several things.) And everything in the story—setting, dialogue, anything else—must be selected by the same principles, both immediate and emblematic interest.

Or one might work, as Chaucer often does, by the obverse of the allegorical method, choosing traditional allegorical emblems (the rose, the lamb, the crown, the grail) and exploring them in quasi-realistic terms. Thus, for example, a literal-minded, practical philosopher—an inventor of household appliances, or a complaints-department supervisor—might find himself in the company of the dying Fisher King. By either of the basic allegorical methods, the writer thinks out first what he wants to say in general, then translates his ideas into people, places, objects, and events, and then, in the process of writing, follows out suggestions that rise from his story, perhaps saying more than he at first thought he had to say.

Expressionistic and surreal fiction is superficially like allegory, but the meaning is much less imposed from without. The expressionist translates some basic psychological reality to actuality: Gregor Samsa becomes not *like* a cockroach but a cockroach, and the story develops, from that point on, realistically. In surreal fiction the writer translates an entire sequence of psychological events, developing his story as the mind spins out dreams. Plotting the story, in either of these modes, is essentially like plotting a realistic piece. The writer shows us dramatically all that we need to know (within the mode) to follow the story to its climax. He does not simply tell us things but dramatizes all that is crucial to our belief in the climax.

We saw earlier how the writer works back from a climax (Helen's surprise) to discover what materials he must dramatize to make the climax meaningful and convincing. In the case of the Helen of Troy story, certain basic facts are given by legend and archeological evidence (what the Trojans were like, what the Achaians were like), and the writer is to some extent stuck with those facts. If he changes things too noticeably, the reader may feel that the writer has made things too easy for himself—playing tennis without the net, as Robert Frost said of poetry without rhyme. Working with a well-known traditional story, or working with material we can find in the newspapers, the writer automatically raises the expectation that we will get not only an interesting story but an interpretation of the facts that we too know—an interpretation that must convince us, if it is to hold our full interest. Theoretically the writer may violate this principle; by tone and style he may establish at once that he is treating the story as a fable from which he can withdraw at any time. Italo Calvino's comic tale of life at the end of the dinosaur age, "The Dinosaurs," is a special case of the well-known event reinterpreted. Because of Calvino's way of telling the story—and also because mutation is a part of the subject— we are not shocked but delighted when the narrator, a dinosaur, surprisingly concludes: "I traveled through valleys and plains. I came to a station, caught the first train, and was lost in the crowd." But though the rule is not firm, it is generally true that old stories retold get much of their interest from our pleasure in the writer's interpretation.

Let us look at how the writer works when he plots backward from the climax of a story that is entirely made up. Any event that seems to the given writer startling, curious, or interest-laden can form the climax of a possible story: A roadside vendor's pickup is struck by a transcontinental tractor-trailer; a woman purposely runs over a flagman on the street. Depending on the complexity of the writer's way of seeing the event— depending, that is, on how much background he feels our understanding of the event requires—the climax becomes the high point of a short story, a novella, or a novel. Since plotting is ordinarily no hasty process but something the writer broods and labors over, trying out one approach, then another, carrying the idea around with him, musing on it casually as he drifts off to sleep, writers often find that an idea for a short story may change into an idea for a novella or even a novel. But for convenience here, let us treat the two climaxes I've mentioned—the wreck of the roadside vendor's pickup and the woman's attack on the flagman—as ideas that remain short-story ideas.

A roadside vendor's pickup is hit by a transcontinental tractor-trailer. Let us say the vendor is the story's central character. In any climax in which the central character is in conflict with something else (another character, some animal, or some more or less impersonal force), the climactic encounter may come about either through the knowledge and volition of both parties or by significant accident. (Accident without significance is boring.) The semi driver may hit the pickup on purpose, accidentally, or for some reason we do not know because we lack access to his thoughts. If the semi driver hits the pickup on purpose, the writer working back from the climax is logically required to show dramatically, in earlier scenes, (1) what each of the two focal characters is like; (2) why the semi driver hits the vendor's pickup. (The writer might conceivably get around both 1 and 2, telling us only what the vendor is like; but the introduction of a malevolent semi driver who simply happens into the story, bringing on the climax, has become such a cliché in modern fiction as to be almost unusable.) The story containing 1 and 2 is a relatively easy kind of story to think out and write, which is not to say that it cannot be an excellent story if well done. The value of the standard feud story always depends on the writer's ability to create powerfully convincing characters in irreconcilable conflict, both sides in some measure sympathetic—that is, both sides pursuing real, though mutually exclusive, values. For the climax to be persuasive, we must be shown dramatically why each character believes what he does and why each cannot sympathize with the values of his antagonist; and we must be shown dramatically why the conflicting characters cannot or do not simply avoid each other, as in real life even tigers ordinarily do. For the climax to be not only persuasive but interesting, it must come about in a way that seems both inevitable and surprising. (In a form as standard as the feud story, this last is exceedingly important.) Needless to say, no surprise will be convincing if it rests on chance, however common chance may be in life.

If the semi driver hits the pickup by accident or for some reason we never learn, the construction of an aesthetically valid story is more difficult, since the value conflict that propels the story must be derived entirely from the central character and his situation. In this case the semi driver functions as an impersonal force and can have only such meaning as the roadside vendor projects onto him; in other words, the semi must be, for the vendor, a symbol. Let us say that for the vendor transcontinental trucks represent power and freedom, a symbolic contrast with his own life, which he views as constricted and unsatisfying. The wreck of the pickup, then, will be grimly ironic. Having thought it out this far, we find that the story begins to fall into place. The story's principle of profluence might be a movement from greatest constriction to least constriction—a development abruptly reversed when the semi hits the pickup.

Say the roadside vendor is a redneck bottom-land farmer, a grower of melons, pumpkins, squash, pole beans, yams, and tomatoes in the red-clay country of Kentucky, southern Missouri, or southern Illinois—a man called Pigtoe. (This version of the plot comes from the writer Leigh Wilson.) Constrictions are easy to find for such a man, betrayed by the land, the government, the newly liberalized Baptist Church, perhaps betrayed by life in other ways as well, at least in his own view: His wife, Alice, is worn and haggard, sickly—other men, like his neighbor Pinky Hearns, have healthy, strong wives, good workers. And Pigtoe's children are too numerous (or not numerous enough, choose one) and rebellious.

The writer might lead up to the climax with three relatively short but texturally rich, at least moderately southern gothic scenes. In the first, Pigtoe is at breakfast with his wife, talking, while outside the children load the truck. The writer can quickly and easily establish Pigtoe's feeling of being squeezed by life—his feelings about the church, the school, blacks, his children and neighbors, taxes, and the weather. But whereas his family is pretty much stuck on the farm, as they are grumblingly aware, Pigtoe can at least get away a little, see the larger world, meet strangers, selling produce from the back of his pickup, out by the highway. The scene ends with Pigtoe watching as his children finish their careless loading.

A brief transitional scene might show Pigtoe driving down Lipes Ridge Road (or whatever) toward the junction of the state highway and the interstate. We get some of Pigtoe's thoughts, sharp images of how he drives the truck, and above all a dramatized movement from one world to another. Then the third scene might show Pigtoe with two or three significant customers—a trim suburban housewife, for instance; a university couple—"hippies," to Pigtoe (they might envy his life "close to the land"); perhaps also a well-off family of blacks in a new Chevy wagon. Through all this and, subtly, from the beginning of the story, we get Pigtoe's feelings about the people around him: his contempt and bitterness, and his envy, almost worship, of the people who have escaped his imprisonment, the men who drive the chrome eighteen-wheelers. Now the climax is set up.

How the writer comes out of it (in the denouement), the writer must probably discover as he writes and repeatedly revises the story. Pigtoe may be killed, or he may be left staring at the tipped-over pickup, honeydews and pumpkins rumbling down the highway toward Oklahoma. Again, the semi driver might stop (not at all the supremely free being Pigtoe has imagined him); Pigtoe in his rage might seize the old red gas-can from the pickup and try—successfully or with pitiful ineptitude —to burn the eighteen-wheeler. Or any of a dozen other things might happen. The writer must decide for himself, discovering his ending from within the story.

The risks in this story we've outlined are apparent. The good writer will think them out carefully before he starts. The main one, of course, is that the story's southern gothicism will seem old hat. The fact that the story is of a standard type is no reason not to write it, however. All fiction is derivative, a fact that the good writer turns to his advantage, making the most of the reader's expectations, twisting old conventions, satisfying expectations in unexpected ways. Because his material is so obviously southern gothic, the writer might choose a style not usual in such fiction, a style as far as possible from that of Flannery O'Connor, Eudora Welty, or William Faulkner. Mainly, however, he must see the material with a fresh eye, using his own experience of southern life, choosing details no other writer has noticed or, anyway, emphasized, thus creating a reality as different from that of gothic convention as gothic convention is from reality itself.

Our second story situation, the woman who purposely runs over a flagman, is the opposite of our Pigtoe story, since here the focal character is the aggressor, not (as at the end of the Pigtoe story) the victim. What the writer must figure out, to justify the climax, is (1) what kind of woman would run over a traffic flagman, and (2) why? Either she can know the flagman and have something personal against him, or she may not know him, but sees him as a symbol—a male chauvinist, for instance. I am ignoring, for my convenience, the possibility that the woman might run over the flagman by accident, mainly because in that case we are almost certainly saddled with a victim story. What precedes the climax would necessarily be a set of harassing events that explain the woman's carelessness. At best the story would be, in the abstract, a duplication of our Pigtoe story: The woman believes one thing—that a certain attitude and way of behaving are effective—and is proved wrong by events.

Let us say, arbitrarily (though in fact the given writer's

choice would not be arbitrary but guided by his intuition of what would make a good story), that the woman does not know the flagman. What central character shall we choose—for example: a harried, unhappy housewife, a tough female executive, a stripper? Any choice could make a good story, but let's take the stripper, an idea that might appeal to a given writer at least partly because of our present stage of social consciousness: No writer before our own moment would be likely to see the stripper in quite the way we do. What pressure can we put on our stripper that will account for the climactic event?

Let us say that our stripper, Fanny, is thirty-six, well-preserved, even beautiful, but hard put to compete with younger strippers of the new breed. She's an old-style stripper, the kind who teases and scorns her male audience, as if taunting them, asking to be tamed—a classic act (she's been the star for years), but her act, like her body, is slipping. Her act is of the highly polished kind: She unclothes slowly, tormentingly, with artistic style. She has, let us say, trained white doves who fly away with each article of clothing she takes off. The younger strippers, who are beginning to challenge her top billing, are new-style strippers. Nakedness means nothing to them—they take off their clothes as indifferently as trees drop leaves—and their acts, because of their easy and uninhibited sexuality, have no need of high artifice or polish. Whereas Fanny grew up in Texas, of stern, southern Baptist stock, and fled to burlesque in troubled defiance, guiltily but brazenly, the new breed grew up in cities like San Francisco and feels no such inner conflict.

Having worked out this general approach to his story, the writer is ready to start figuring out his scenes. By the rule of elegance and efficiency, he will choose the smallest number of scenes possible—perhaps three. First, the writer might use a scene in which Fanny, fearfully and angrily, watches the rehearsal of a younger stripper's act. She can tell as she watches that, though the act is technically shoddy beside her own, it is being groomed as a starring act and may well push her from her billing. In the next scene, Fanny might confront the manager or director and learn from him that her suspicions are well-founded. She goes into a rage. At the peak of this scene she might slap the director, and he, to her shock and amazement, might slap her back, even fire her. In the third scene, Fanny drives toward the flagman, who unluckily smiles a trifle lewdly at her, bringing on the climax. What happens after this—the story's denouement or pull-away—the writer may know only when he writes it. (Some writers claim they know the last lines of their stories from the beginning. I think this is usually a bad idea, producing fiction that is subtly forced, or mechanical.)

This brief, rough sketch of a possible story raises an extremely important point—a point as fundamental, for the most serious kind of writer, as the concept of the uninterruptible fictional dream. What we have so far, in the sketch we've worked out—and what many quite good writers never go beyond—is a projected piece of fiction that, if well-written, will be no more than a persuasive imitation of reality. It shows how things happen and may imply certain values, but it does not look hard at the meaning of things. It has no real theme. This is a common limitation of second-rate fiction and may sometimes characterize even quite powerful fiction, like Eudora Welty's novel *Losing Battles*. We get an accurate and totally convincing picture of what it feels like to have a death in the family, what it is like to leave one's husband and children for a new "free" life, how it feels to be sued for malpractice or to lose an election; we do not get close examination of some deep-rooted idea. The writer, in other words, has done the first job done in all serious fiction—he has created a convincing and illuminating sequence of events— but he has not done the second, which is to "mine deeper!" as Melville says, dig out the fundamental meaning of events by organizing the imitation of reality around some primary question or theme suggested by the character's concern.

The theme of our story about Fanny the stripper might be, of course, male chauvinism; or it might be Art versus Life (or

Nature); or nakedness in all its forms. The writer's choice of theme, partly Fanny's choice, will dictate his selection and organization of details, his style, and so forth. For instance, if what seems to him central in Fanny's struggle has to do with the contrast between Art and Nature, he will focus carefully on the difference between Fanny's act and that of the younger girls, summoning imagery, etc., that subtly underscores his point of focus. He may pay close attention to Fanny's mirror, a beautifully carpentered object with a history and, for Fanny, special meaning. And the flagman's way of doing his job—negligently and artlessly, or officiously and carefully—will have bearing on the climax. If the theme the writer chooses is nakedness, he will choose other details to brood on and develop—the chipping paint on the dressing-room walls, for instance; the psychological nakedness of some character; the manager's unwillingness to disguise or cover over his lack of interest in Fanny's well-being or, if it comes to that, his hatred of all she represents. Given this theme, the writer may find himself introducing a decorous old janitor who clothes his every mood in the most painstaking etiquette and who wears, whatever the weather, two sweaters and a coat. These become the "counters," so to speak, for the writer's thought: They help him find out and express precisely what he means.

Theme, it should be noticed, is not imposed on the story but evoked from within it—initially an intuitive but finally an intellectual act on the part of the writer. The writer muses on the story idea to determine what it is in it that has attracted him, why it seems to him worth telling. Having determined that what interests him—and what chiefly concerns the major character— is the idea of nakedness (physical, psychological, perhaps spiritual), he toys with various ways of telling his story, thinks about what has been said before about nakedness (for instance, in traditional Christianity and pagan myth), broods on every image that occurs to him, turning it over and over, puzzling on it, hunting for connections, trying to figure out—before he

writes, while he writes, and in the process of repeated revisions
—what it is he really thinks. (How naked should we be or can
we be? Is openness, vulnerability, a virtue or a defect? To what
extent, with what important qualifications?) He finds himself
bringing in black strippers, perhaps an Indian stripper, supported by imagery that recalls primitive nakedness. And so on.
Only when he thinks out his story in this way does he achieve
not just an alternative reality or, loosely, an imitation of nature,
but true, firm art—fiction as serious thought.

I have said that a writer may also plot a piece of fiction by
working his way forward from an initial situation. Say he gets
the slightly lunatic idea of a young Chinese teacher of highschool English in San Francisco who is kidnapped by a group of
Chinese thugs because they want him to write their story, of
which they're inordinately proud. If the fiction is not to be a
victim story (hence unusable), some conflict must be established: The teacher must be given a will of his own and a purpose opposed to that of his captors. In other words, he must
want—in some desperately serious way—not to write their
story. What, we ask, groping toward a story, would make our
teacher so unwilling to write the exploits of the thugs that he
would cross them, understanding the danger? Perhaps he has
his head full of the legends of Mongolian bandits, and perhaps
he's not only a teacher but an ambitious, fiercely dedicated
young poet, steeped in the tradition of Chinese poetry and
prose. In this case, the story of a miserable gang that does nothing more lofty than knock over an occasional Savings & Loan
Association may be a story that so outrages his sense of life
and art that he refuses to have anything to do with it. If the
gang simply shoots him for his recalcitrance, that's the end of
that; no story. How can we keep him alive and thus keep the
story going? Perhaps he does write as they tell him to do, but
writes insultingly, legitimately contrasting the petty escapades
of his kidnappers with the exploits of great Mongolian bandits.
Insofar as his captors are persuaded that they really ought to be

more like Mongolian bandits—and they would not have kidnapped him and asked him to write if they didn't have some pride—the kidnappers may spare him, grudgingly, learning from him a more dazzling kind of banditry. Eventually, then, it might occur to them that, given rush-hour traffic in downtown San Francisco, thieves might rob a bank and escape if they were mounted on horses, like Mongolian bandits. So we might lead to the comic-heroic image of modern Mongolian bandits clattering across the Golden Gate Bridge in traditional regalia.

The writer's basic problems when he thinks forward from an initial situation are essentially the same as when he thinks backward from a climax. As his plot line takes shape and he gradually makes out what his climax or series of climaxes is to be, he must figure out what he must dramatically prove to make the climax or series meaningful and convincing. He must figure out his theme—in this case, clearly, the relationship between art and life, and the moral responsibility of the artist. He must work out major details of characterization and think out what some of his major images imply (the extent, that is, to which they function as symbols); he must work out his story's natural length and rhythm and decide on the appropriate style.

So far we've talked mainly about short-story plotting. Let us look now at longer forms; that is, the novella and the novel. I will treat at length only energeic plots, since for long works those are the kind most likely to succeed.

The novella can be defined only as a work shorter than a novel (most novellas run somewhere between 30,000 and 50,000 words) and both longer and more episodic than a short story. I use the word "episodic" loosely here, meaning only that the novella usually has a series of climaxes, each more intense than the last, though it may be built—and perhaps in fact ought to be built—of one continuous action. William Gass's "The Pedersen Kid" is a more or less perfect example of the form. Discounting brief flashbacks which show what Big Hans (the hired man), Pa, and Ma were like before the opening of the central action and how they came to be the people they are now, the action is a continuous stream moving through a series of climaxes, focused throughout on a single character, young Jorge. The story runs as follows: In some desolate rural land-scape (Wisconsin, perhaps North Dakota), in the dead of winter, a neighbor's child, the Pedersen kid, arrives and is dis-covered almost frozen to death near Jorge's father's barn; when he's brought in and revived, he tells of the murderer at his house, a man with yellow gloves; Big Hans and Pa decide to go there, taking young Jorge; when they get there, Jorge, making a dash from the barn to the house, hears shots; Big Hans and Pa are killed, apparently—Jorge is not sure—and Jorge slips inside the house and down cellar, where at the end of the novella he is still waiting. The stream of action is complete and uninter-rupted, from the initial situation (the cause of the sequence of events; that is, the arrival of the Pedersen kid with his strange story, challenging the courage and humanity of Big Hans and Pa) to the closing event, Jorge's recognition that he has done what he must, has kept his word and so has achieved identity, or human status. But the continuous stream nevertheless has its progression of increasingly powerful climaxes, each, if we look closely, symbolic and ritualistic as well as intense on the level of pure action. The writer, in other words, has organized his con-tinuous action as a group of scenes or scene-cluster segments, loosely, "episodes."

The blocking of Gass's novella might be laid out as follows:

The Pedersen kid arrives and is brought into the kitchen and there thawed out or "resurrected" by Jorge's mother. (Here, as throughout the novel, suggestions of mystic ritual abound. Ma works on the frozen Pedersen kid as she works when baking bread. The boy's whiteness reminds Jorge of flour, and Ma works on him, kneading him, on the kitchen table, where cus-tomarily she kneads her breaddough. Notice, by the way, how thoroughly realistic all this is, for all its symbolic freighting. The details of the scene have the sharp-edged vividness of Edward Weston photographs or realistic painting. Yet nearly every detail works symbolically as well as literally.)

For the thawing of the boy, Ma needs some of Pa's whiskey (an ironic permutation of the wine that goes with eucharistic bread, the Pedersen kid's "dead" body), and we learn what a dangerous, mean drunkard Pa is, a man both violent and spiritually debased, snakelike, capable of dumping the contents of his bedpan on Big Hans' head. The scene began with intense pressure (the whole family is slightly crazy: Ma trembles in fear of Pa; Jorge resists, almost psychotically, the thawing of the kid found in the snow) and builds urgently to the novella's first climax, Big Hans' challenge of Pa and the decision to go to the Pedersens' house and look for the man with yellow gloves.

Having, in effect, vowed to do so, Pa, Big Hans, and Jorge set out, armed and angrily tormenting one another, and, on their way to the Pedersens', find the murderer's dead horse, nearly buried in snow. (Throughout the novella, snow-burial and spring resurrection are seminal ideas.) Their discovery of the horse—and the loss of Pa's whiskey—brings on the second climax: Because they've said they'll go to the Pedersens' and are too stubborn to back down, Pa and Big Hans confirm their resolve. They make it to the Pedersens', Jorge reaches the wall of the house, and (in the novella's third main climax) Pa and Big Hans are shot by someone inside. Rather than freeze to death, though he expects to be killed anyway, Jorge goes inside. The novella's final climax is Jorge's recognition of what it is that he has achieved, whether or not he will live to tell of it.

"The Pedersen Kid" is, I've said, a more or less perfect example of the novella form—a single stream of action focused on one character and moving through a series of increasingly intense climaxes. We find the same structure in many of the novellas of Henry James—"The Turn of the Screw" and "The Jolly Corner," for instance—and in the work of various other writers:

Flaubert in "A Simple Heart," Gide in "Theseus" and "The Pastoral Symphony," William Faulkner in "The Bear," and several of the novellas of Thomas Mann. Though this form of the novella is the most elegant and efficient novella structure, it is not the only structure possible, however. Some novella writers write, in effect, baby novels, shifting from one point of view (or focal character) to another and using true episodes, with time breaks between, instead of a continuous stream of action. D. H. Lawrence, in his novella "The Fox," uses this more complicated form with some success. The choice makes it possible for him to cover a longer span of time than is customary in the novella and also a greater latitude of style. One pays for these advantages in that the progress of events has less urgency than Gass and Faulkner achieve, while the brevity of the work prohibits his achieving the powerhouse effect usual in the final section of a good full-length novel.

Another possible structure is fictional pointillism, used interestingly in Robert Coover's "Hansel and Gretel" and masterfully by William Gass in what is to date probably his finest work, "In the Heart of the Heart of the Country." In this form the writer lets out his story in snippets, sometimes called "crots," moving as if at random from one point to another, gradually amassing the elements, literal and symbolic, of a quasi-energeic action. No rule governs the organization of such a work but that the writer be a prose-poet of genius. Even if he has some intellectual system for arranging his crots, the basic principle of his assembly is feeling: He shuffles and reshuffles his fragments to find the most moving of possible presentations, and he achieves his climaxes not, as in linear fiction, by the gelling of key events, but by poetic force. Depending, as it does, so largely on texture —having abandoned structure in the traditional sense (events causally related and presented more or less in sequence)—the mode runs the great risk of overrichness, the writer's tendency to push too hard, producing an effect of sentimentality. The great advantage, on the other hand, is the necessary focus on imagery whereby repeated images accrue greater and greater psychological and symbolic force.

A good novella, whatever its structure, has an effect analogous to that of the tone poem in music. A good novel, on the other hand, has an effect more like that of a Beethoven symphony. Let me try to make these analogies a little clearer.

The chief beauty of a novella is its almost oriental purity, its elegant tracing of an emotional line. Whereas the short story moves to an "epiphany," as Joyce said—in other words to a climactic moment of recognition or understanding on the part of the central character or, at least, the reader—achieving its effect by fully justifying, through authenticating background, its climactic event or moment, the novella moves through a series of small epiphanies or secondary climaxes to a much more firm conclusion. Through the sparest means possible—not through the amassing of the numerous forces that operate in a novel but by following out a single line of thought—the novella reaches an end wherein the world is, at least for the central character, radically changed. Jorge, if he ever gets home again, will be a different young man: He has survived and triumphed in his rite of passage, has achieved his adult identity. The "fox" at the end of D. H. Lawrence's novella has won his woman and murdered his enemy. The bear, at the end of Faulkner's novella, is gone, and Ike McCaslin is changed forever. Nothing can be more perfect or complete than a good novella. When a novel achieves the same glassy perfection—as does Flaubert's *Madame Bovary*— we may tend to find it dissatisfying, untrue. The "perfect" novel lacks the richness and raggedness of the best long fictions. We need not go into the reasons for this except to notice that the novella normally treats one character and one important action in his life, a focus that lends itself to neat cut-offs, framing. The novel, on the other hand, at least makes some pretense of imitating the world in all its complexity; we not only look closely at various characters, we hear rumors of distant wars and marriages, we glimpse characters whom, like people on the subway, we will never see again. As a result, too much neatness in a novel kills the novel's fundamental effect. When all of a novel's strings are too neatly tied together at the end, as sometimes happens in Dickens and almost always happens in the popular mystery thriller, we feel the novel to be unlifelike. The novel is by definition, to some extent at least, a "loose, baggy monster"— as Henry James said irritably, disparaging the novels of Tolstoy. It cannot be too loose, too baggy or monstrous; but a novel built as prettily as a teacup is not of much use.

A novel is like a symphony in that its closing movement echoes and resounds with all that has gone before. This is rare in the novella; the effect requires too much time, too much mass. Toward the close of a novel, the writer brings back— directly or in the form of his characters' recollections—images, characters, events, and intellectual motifs encountered earlier. Unexpected connections begin to surface; hidden causes become plain; life becomes, however briefly and unstably, organized; the universe reveals itself, if only for the moment, as inexorably moral; the outcome of the various characters' actions is at last manifest; and we see the responsibility of free will. It is this closing orchestration that the novel exists for. If such a close does not come, for whatever theoretically good reason, we shut the book with feelings of dissatisfaction, as if cheated. This is of course tantamount to saying that the novel, as a genre, has a built-in metaphysic. And so it does. The writer who does not accept the metaphysic can never write a novel; he can only play off it, as Beckett and Barthelme do, achieving his own effects by visibly subverting those traditional to the novel, working like the sculptor who makes sculptures that self-destruct or the composer who dynamites pianos. I am not saying, of course, that the artist ought to lie, only that in the long run the anti-novelist is probably doomed to at least relative failure because we do not believe him. We are not profoundly moved by Homer, Shakespeare, or Melville because we would *like* to believe the metaphysical assumptions their fictions embody—an orderly universe that imposes moral responsibility—but because we do believe those assumptions. We cannot—except in very subtle ways—believe both Homer and Samuel Beckett.

Successful novel-length fictions can be organized in numerous ways: energeically, that is, by a sequence of causally related events; juxtapositionally, when the novel's parts have symbolic or thematic relationship but no flowing development through cause and effect; or lyrically, that is, by some essentially musical principle—one thinks, for example, of the novels of Marcel Proust or Virginia Woolf.

The lyrical novel is the most difficult to talk about. What carries the reader forward is not plot, basically—though the novel may contain, in disguised form, a sequence of causally related events—but some form of rhythmic repetition: a key image or cluster of images (the ocean, a childhood memory of a swingset, a snow-capped mountain, a forest); a key event or group of events, to which the writer returns repeatedly, then leaves for material that increasingly deepens and redefines the meaning of the event or events; or some central idea or cluster of ideas. The form lends itself to psychological narrative, imitating the play of the wandering or dreaming mind (especially the mind troubled by one or more traumatic experiences); and most practitioners of this form of the novel create works with a marked dream-like quality. The classic example is *Finnegans Wake*. A more manageable example is John Hawkes' powerful and mysterious early novel, *The Beetle-Leg*, a nightmare story in which the narrative moves with increasing speed and pressure from one to another of a few key images—a beetle-leg-sized crack in the wall of a dam, a motorcycle gang, and so forth.

The most common form of the novel is energeic. This is both the simplest and the hardest kind of novel to write—the simplest because it's the most inevitable and self-propelled, the hardest because it's by far the hardest to fake. By his made-up word *energeia*, as we've said, Aristotle meant "the actualization of the potential that exists in character and situation." (The fact that Aristotle was talking about Greek tragedy need not delay us. If he'd known about novels, he'd have said much the same.) Logically, the energeic novel falls into three parts, Aristotle's "beginning, middle, and end," which we may think of as roughly equal in length and which fall into the pattern exposition, development, and denouement. In practice, no sane novelist would devote the first third of his total number of pages to exposition, the second third to development, and the last to denouement, if only because exposition has no profluence, and after five or ten pages the reader would quit. It is for this reason that Aristotle recommends that the writer begin "in the middle of things" and fill in the exposition as he can. But for purposes of discussion it will be useful to treat the three components separately.

In his exposition, the writer presents all that the reader will need to know about character and situation, the potential to be "actualized." Obviously he cannot plan his exposition without a clear idea of what the development section is to contain and at least some inkling of what will happen in the denouement, since in the novel, as in the short story or novella, what the reader needs to know is everything that is necessary if he is to believe and understand the ensuing action. If the plot is to be elegant, not sloppy and inefficient, then for the ensuing action the reader must know the full set of causes and (essentially) nothing else; that is, no important information in the exposition should be irrelevant to the action that ensues. And here, as in the shorter forms, what the reader learns in the exposition he must be shown through dramatic events, not told. (It is not enough that we be authorially informed that a character is vicious beyond belief. We must see him slit a baby's throat.) Finally, if anything is to come of the initial situation and characterization, the matter presented in the exposition, the situation must be somehow unstable: The character must for some reason feel compelled to act, effecting some change, and he must be shown to be a character capable of action.

This means, in effect, that in the relationship between character and situation there must be some conflict: Certain forces, within and outside the character, must press him toward a certain course of action, while other forces, both within and outside, must exert strong pressure against that course of action. Both pressures must come not only from outside the character but also from within him, because otherwise the conflict involves no doubt, no moral choice, and as a result can have no profound meaning. (All meaning, in the best fiction, comes from —as Faulkner said—the heart in conflict with itself. All true suspense, we have said, is a dramatic representation of the anguish of moral choice.) The famous Fichtean curve is in effect a diagram of this conflict situation:

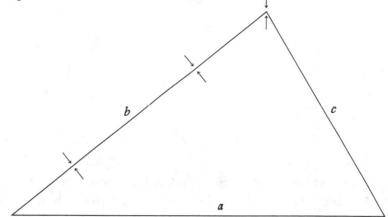

Let line *a* represent the "normal" course of action; that is, the course the character would take if he cared only for safety and stability and so did not assert his independent will, trying the difficult or impossible in the hope of effecting change. Let line *b* represent the course of action our character does take, struggling against odds and braving conflict. The descending arrows (↓) represent forces (enemies, custom, or natural law) that work against the character's will, and the ascending arrows (↑) represent forces that support him in his enterprise. The peak of the ascending line (*b*) represents the novel's climactic moment; and line *c* represents all that follows—that is, the denouement: The

conflict is now resolved, or in the process of resolving, either because the will of the central character has been overwhelmed or
because he has won and his situation is once more stabilizing. A
chart of the novel's emotional development (our feeling of suspense, fascination, or anxiety as we read) is, then, Fichte's curve.
Since the ascending action is in fact not smooth but moves
through a series of increasingly intense climaxes (the episodic
rhythm of the novel), a refined version of the curve might be
the following:

I was told many years ago, I forget by whom, the plot of a
novel-in-progress that perfectly illustrates all this. The central
character is a keen-witted, tough young Apache Indian—let us
call him Jim—who spent his early years on the Indian reservation but has now earned a degree in American anthropology
from the University of California at Berkeley. His mother is old
and in need of his financial help, and his younger brother needs
money for college (he wants to be, say, a Methodist minister).
Jobs in our hero's field are scarce, but he manages to land one,
without interview, in a small university in Ohio—let us call it
Twin Oaks—formerly a teachers' college. At Twin Oaks a program in Indian studies is just being established, supported by a
federal grant. Jim loads his few possessions on his Harley-
Davidson and travels to Ohio, where he discovers that a terrible

mistake has been made: What Twin Oaks University thinks it is getting is a specialist in *Asian* Indian studies. No one knows yet that Jim is an Apache and a specialist in American Indians— urban ones at that. What to do? The "normal" course of action would be to ride back to Berkeley and try again. The more daring course of action is to make an attempt to fake it as an Asian Indian. He gets himself a turban. Now the writer's business is to put pressure on his hero and also to line up those who will encourage and abet him, on one hand, and those who will oppose him, on the other. We have reached what we may call the development section.

The writer arranges a set of crises for his hero. Another Apache may come to give a lecture, or a real Asian Indian may arrive. A faculty member may develop a powerful dislike for our hero and for some reason may take to spying on him, trying to get him fired. Certain students may grow suspicious; or his brother, overzealous in piety, may come to visit; or a woman he goes to bed with may hear him talking in his sleep and suspect his secret. At the same time, the writer arranges forces on the hero's side—friendly students and fellow teachers, increasing pressures from home that force our hero to keep going (his mother breaks her hip and has greater need of money), and so on. Finally the novel's main climax comes, and the conflict is in one way or another resolved, moving the novel into its denouement. (Here the diagram can be slightly misleading. The denouement may be a winding down of the action, a return to rest, or it may be high-pitched, as in the case of a triumphant closing section or a closing section that is terrible and dark—for example, the hero burns down the university and many people die. Either way, the conflict is resolved; our initial concern, the keeping of the secret, changes to something else—the result of the secret's having been discovered.)

When he knows what is to happen in his development section, and something of what it means philosophically (thematically), the writer is ready to work out the details of his exposition. If the action requires Jim to have a violent streak, we must be shown dramatically how this violent streak developed. If he forms a friendship with one of the deans because they both play the cornet, we must hear where and how Jim learned to play. Or, to put it generally, the writer must show us everything of importance to Jim's character and everything of importance about his situation, which means mainly the character of all those who will support or oppose him at Twin Oaks U, their political affiliations and biases, everything about them that will have some bearing on the action.

This exposition, we've said, cannot be set down all in a lump at the beginning of the book. If the story is to be profluent, the action must get going almost immediately, and the writer must slip in exposition as he can, the only limit being that by the time we reach the peak of the Fichtean curve there should be no more exposition to be presented. When a novel's denouement has been properly set up, it falls like an avalanche, and the writer's chief job is to describe stone by stone how it falls. Having worked out what he must present in his exposition and development sections, the writer comes to the most difficult part of his plotting, what medieval rhetoricians called *dispositio*, the disposition or organization of the various materials he has selected.

In theory the writer may decide to start his action anywhere, but in practice his options are limited. If he starts too far back (with Jim in his first year of college, say), the novel will be slow starting and almost certainly tedious; and if he starts too near the end—for instance, with the novel's dramatic last event—the result will look gimmicky and self-regarding. The writer who wishes to avoid such faults as mannerism and frigidity will figure out where the action actually begins—probably with Jim's arrival at Twin Oaks—and start there. (Thus Homer—to shift for a moment to the sublime—begins not with the opening of the Trojan war, not even with Agamemnon's seizing of Briseus, but with the argument of Achilles and Agamemnon, the argument that shows the contrast between Agamemnon's cynicism and Achilles' extreme idealism, the argument that sets off Achilles' withdrawal from the war and will ultimately bring down tragedy on his head.) Having decided where he will start, the writer then plans his rhythmical climaxes, then figures out in detail where he will work in the necessary exposition. At every stage of his work, the writer may revise his earlier plan. He may discover, for example, that he needs more time for exposition in chapter 2, and he may therefore insert some new minor climax, with a trough on each side of it, giving himself more room.

I will leave it to the reader to figure out the plotting of the enormous cousin of the energeic novel, the so-called architectonic novel; that is, a novel with two or more parallel energeic plots, each focused on a central character or group of characters. (This was a favorite form of the Victorians, not to mention Tolstoy, and can still be used, as William Gaddis proves in *JR*.) All the plots must be philosophically related. Think, for example, of the two main plots of *Anna Karenina*, one leading to Anna's symbolic damnation—her suicide among mumbling voices and sudden, strange light—the other leading to Levin's symbolic and actual salvation. Basically the plotting process is the same as for the simple energeic novel, only harder and also more risky, since too much neatness in the parallel plots may make the novel seem contrived, and too little will make it sprawl, as if out of control. I also leave to the reader the problem of working out the novel that imitates the biographical form (e.g., *David Copperfield*). Here the plotting is energeic, at least for long stretches, but the novel breaks into large episodes from various periods of the hero's life, and the choice of these episodes (as opposed to other possible episodes) follows theme. Again the risks are self-evident. If the thematic connection between the various episodes is too neat, the novel will seem contrived and unlifelike; and if the connections are too vague, the novel may lack focus.

To a large extent, whatever kind of plot he chooses, the writer is more servant than master of his story. He can almost never use important details only once: They are sure to call out for repetition. For instance, if the writer gives the hero a nightmare, a nightmare so well done (as it had better be) that the reader feels something of the character's distress, the writer— and the reader after him—will feel a need for another nightmare later, or some clear equivalent, element calling to element through the novel, form crying out to form. If he introduces a love scene, he commits himself to later developments of that scene; if he focuses closely on a minor character, he commits himself to that character's return, if only as a memory.

It is this quality of the novel, its built-in need to return and repeat, that forms the physical basis of the novel's chief glory, its resonant close. (It also sets up a risk that the novel may seem contrived.) What rings and resounds at the end of a novel is not just physical, however. What moves us is not just that characters, images, and events get some form of recapitulation or recall: We are moved by the increasing connectedness of things, ultimately a connectedness of values. Coleridge pointed out, stirred to the observation by his interest in Hartleian psychology, that increasingly complex systems of association can give a literary work some of its power. When we encounter two things in close association, Hartley noticed, we tend to recall one when we encounter the other. Thus, for example, if one is standing in a drugstore when one first reads Shelley, the next time one goes to a drugstore one may think of the poet, and the next time one encounters a poem by Shelley one may get a faint whiff of Dial and bathsalts. The same thing happens when we read fiction. If the first time our hero meets a given character it occurs in a graveyard, the character's next appearance will carry with it some residue of the graveyard setting.

The effect can be roughly illustrated this way. Let *a* represent a pair of bloody shoes, first encountered at the foot of a willow tree, *b*; let *c* equal an orphan home, first encountered in a thunderstorm, *d*; and let *e* represent a woman's kiss, experienced on a train, *f*. If *a* (the bloody shoes) is mentioned later in the story, it draws with it a memory of the willow (*b* in brackets). In the same way *c* produces [*d*] as an echo, and *e* produces [*f*]. If the top of the line below is the beginning of the narrative and the bottom of the line is the end, then a writer might develop some such pattern of associations as the following:

a	*b*	
[*b*]	*a*	
c	*d*	
[*d*] *c*	*b* [*a*]	
e	*f*	
[*a*] *b*	*c* [*d*]	
[*f*] *e*	*a* [*b*] [*d*]	
[*e*] *f*	*a* *c* [*b*] [*d*]	

Compared to what actually happens in fiction, this diagram is simple and crude in the extreme, but perhaps it makes the point. Even at the end of a short story, the power of an organized return of images, events, and characters can be considerable. Think of Joyce's "The Dead." In the closing moments of a novel the effect can be overwhelming.

We are of course not talking about just any old return of images, etc. The images that come together at the end of "The Dead," each dragging its train of associations, are all images of death. The images and experiences brought together in Molly Bloom's soliloquy in *Ulysses* create an equally symbolic but vastly more complex thought-emotion in which the principle of coherence is loving affirmation against odds associationally recalled. The "yes" that begins as a copulative cry enlarges outward to become a mystical affirmation of all the universe, including even death. To achieve such an effect, the writer must rise above his physical plot to an understanding of all his plot's elements and all their relationships, including those that are inexpressible. The novel's denouement, in other words, is not simply the end of the story but the story's fulfillment. Here at last, emotionally if not intellectually, the reader understands everything and everything is symbolic. This understanding, which the writer must reach before he can make it available to the reader, is impossible to anticipate in the planning of the novel. It is the novelist's reward for thinking carefully about reality, brooding on every image, every action, every word, both those things he planned from the beginning and those that crept in in the service of convincingness. Unfortunately, though the effect of a true denouement can be described, the writing of a good denouement cannot be taught. One can only give hints and warnings. The most useful hint is perhaps this: Read the story over and over, at least a hundred times—literally—watching for subtle meanings, connections, accidental repetitions, psychological significance. Leave nothing—no slightest detail— unexamined; and when you discover implications in some image or event, oonch those implications toward the surface. This may be done in a variety of ways: by introducing subtle repetitions of the image, so that it catches the reader's subliminal attention; by slipping the image into a metaphor that helps to fix and clarify the meaning you have found in it; or by placing the image (or event or whatever) in closer proximity to related symbols. As for the warnings, two are of most importance: On one hand, don't overdo the denouement, so ferociously pushing meaning that the reader is distracted from the fictional dream, giving the narrative a too conscious, contrived, or "workshop" effect; and don't, on the other hand, write so subtly or timidly— from fear of sentimentality or obviousness—that no one, not even the angels aflutter in the rafters, can hear the resonance.

Exercises

One of the best ways of learning to write is by doing exercises. The following group and individual exercises are some I have found helpful, but any teacher or student can think up others just as good. I recommend keeping the exercises in a notebook (a loose-leaf or spring-binder) for reference later, perhaps along with other things useful to the writer—story ideas, impressions, snatches of dialogue, newspaper clippings. Some writers of course find such things more useful than do others. Some write each story from scratch, making everything up; others build more slowly, depending more heavily—as Dostoevsky did—on snippets from their reading, journal entries, and the like.

I. Group Exercises and Questions for Discussion

Many of the individual exercises in section II below work equally well as exercises to be written, read aloud (voluntarily), and discussed in class. One advantage of using them in this way is that students discover how good they all are—no small matter. Once a class discovers that it's very good (and most students, when they work on some limited, clearly defined problem, are surprisingly good), the class becomes exciting. (In my experience, fifteen to twenty minutes is enough class time to spend on the writing, and for writers well beyond the beginner stage, five minutes may be sufficient.) A second advantage of doing individual exercises as class exercises is that the criticism that follows tends to be of the kind most useful to the writer, especially when the course is still young. No one is likely to come down hard on an exercise knocked off in fifteen minutes. A few slips and infelicities are to be expected. So the discussion is of the kind it ought to be. It points out small mistakes, not making too much of them, and focuses on virtues or potential. The third advantage, of course, is instant feedback.

Some of the things that ought to be covered in every course on writing prose fiction can be covered efficiently only by a class working as a group. Exercises of this kind follow. No one class can get through all of them, and it should always be borne in mind by both the teacher and his students that the most important thing that can be done in class, once the basics have been covered, is the reading and criticism of original fiction. Thinking about the exercises can sometimes be as valuable as sitting down to do them. As a rule, it is useful to do certain kinds of exercises—especially those involving plotting—throughout the term, since the skills to be developed by these exercises cannot be acquired all at once. With practice the group and each of its members gets faster and better at doing the job. For most of these exercises, either the teacher or some member of the group will need to act as blackboard recorder and referee. The class will need to recognize the referee's decision as final. Group exercises become chaotic and therefore boring if no one is accepted as the settler of disputes about, for instance, the name and age of the character being made up. It should also go without saying that occasionally some of these exercises might be used not for group discussion but for essays or meditations in the writer's notebook.

1. Create, in oral cooperation, two characters suitable for a ghost story—first the victim (the person frightened or harmed), then the ghost. Work out for these characters the name, age, background, psychological makeup, physical description, family connections, circle of immediate friends, occupation, appropriate setting, and anything else that seems important. In doing this exercise, and all those that follow, do not be unduly clever —for instance, choosing as the two characters here a dog and a lizard. Undue cleverness defeats the purpose of the exercise, raising complex problems before the simple ones have been solved.

2. Write, by oral cooperation, the opening paragraph (a description of setting) for a parodic or serious gothic tale.

3. Write, by oral cooperation, the opening paragraph (a description of the yarn-spinner told in the voice of the poor, dumb credulous narrator) of a comic yarn. Consider using not the traditional yarn-spinner (a backwater Southerner or New Englander) but some interesting variant: a canny old woman, a black, a first-generation Chinese-American.

4. Cooperatively list the customary elements of one or more of the following: a gothic romance, a murder mystery, a yarn, a TV situation comedy, a Western, or some other popular genre with which the whole group is familiar. What are the philosophical implications of each of these elements? For example: The traditional ghost story includes, among other things, some old, remote building, an emphasis on weather (especially wind, cold, and dampness), a restless animal (dog, wolf, owl, bat). What do these elements seem to mean psychologically? What are some possible symbolic meanings of the ghost's return? The genres listed above are all "popular"; that is, their appeal is usually just adventure or entertainment. Suggest ways in which one or more of them might be elevated to serious fiction. How,

for instance, might ghost-story conventions be used to explore the relationship of an independent, domineering mother and her intimidated daughter?

5. Plot a realistic short story, beginning with the climax and working backward. What characters are needed for the climax and what are they like? (See exercise 1, above.) What must be dramatized to authenticate the climax? How many scenes are necessary to achieve the climax?

6. Using the story worked out in exercise 5, divide up the scenes among members of the group and write them, then read aloud and discuss.

7. Plot a realistic story, working forward from an initial situation.

8. Plot a story based on some legend.

9. Plot a comic or serious fable. For examples of the form, see Aesop or James Thurber.

10. Plot an allegorical fiction, beginning with the idea or "message" and translating to persons, places, and things.

11. Plot a short surreal fiction; a short expressionistic fiction.

12. Plot a tale.

13. Plot a realistic or fabulous short story, beginning with three basic symbols (for example, an axe, the moon, a set of golden dentures). Before working out the plot, discuss possible meanings of the symbols. By a "fabulous" story I mean here one containing nonexistent beings or some imaginary and fantastic

place, but a story that, given these oddities, operates realistically; that is, by ordinary, not poetic, cause and effect.

14. Plot a realistic or fabulous story, beginning with the theme, or philosophical subject (for example, loss of innocence, possessive versus selfless love, varieties of courage and cowardice).

15. Discuss ways of giving fiction profluence (forward-movingness) without causally related events. Plot such a story.

16. Plot a story by beginning with a choice of the style to be used. Let the style be in some way odd or unusual—for example, a preponderance of very long sentences, or the use of the virtually unusable second-person point of view.

17. Plot a novella.

18. Plot a novel.

19. Plot an interesting novel on a hackneyed subject; for example, a novel about a circus, a lost valley, a gold mine, an unfaithful wife, a doomed planet, first love.

20. Plot an architectonic (or multi-plot) novel; plot a novel that imitates the form of the biography (*David Copperfield*).

II. Individual Exercises
for the Development of Technique

It is not necessary that a beginning writer do all—or any—of these exercises, and it would be impossible, as well as wasteful, for a student to do all of them in one term, since the exercises should not be substituted for the writing of actual short stories, tales, fables, yarns, sketches, novellas, or novels. One of the most important things a writer can learn is the feeling from within of a complete fictional form; so the student should work on the exercises only during the early weeks of the course and thereafter only at odd moments, putting most of his effort into complete pieces of fiction, preferably short forms, then longer forms.

The point of these technical exercises is this: Most apprentice writers underestimate the difficulty of becoming artists; they do not understand or believe that great writers are usually those who, like concert pianists, know many ways of doing everything they do. Knowledge is no substitute for genius; but genius supported by vast technique makes a literary master. Especially just now, when competition for publication is probably greater than ever before, it is helpful for a writer to know technique.

Any apprentice writer who does at least some of these exercises faithfully and well will see that when he gets to, say, exercise 20, he is in a position to do the early exercises with much more facility than when he began; and every exercise faithfully performed will teach a technique useful in short or long fiction. The writer who has worked hard at these exercises will see, whenever he writes a story or novel, that he has various choices available at every point in his fiction, and he will be in a better position to choose the best—or invent something new.

The exercises should be approached, then, with the utmost seriousness. Every true apprentice writer has, however he may try to keep it secret even from himself, only one major goal: glory. The shoddy writer wants only publication. He fails to recognize that almost anyone willing to devote between twelve and fourteen hours a day to writing—and there are many such people—will eventually get published. But only the great writer will survive—the writer who fully understands his trade and is willing to take time and the necessary risks—always assuming, of course, that the writer is profoundly honest and, at least in his writing, sane.

Sanity in a writer is merely this: However stupid he may be in his private life, he never cheats in writing. He never forgets that his audience is, at least ideally, as noble, generous, and tolerant as he is himself (or more so), and never forgets that he is writing about people, so that to turn characters to cartoons, to treat his characters as innately inferior to himself, to forget their reasons for being as they are, to treat them as brutes, is bad art. Sanity in a writer also involves taste. The true writer has a great advantage over most other people: He knows the great tradition of literature, which has always been the cutting edge of morality, religion, and politics, to say nothing of social reform. He knows what the greatest literary minds of the past are proud to do and what they will not stoop to, and his knowledge informs his practice. He fits himself to the company he most respects and enjoys: the company of Homer, Vergil, Dante, Shakespeare, and so forth. Their standards become, in some measure, his own. Pettiness, vulgarity, bad taste fall away from him automatically, and when he reads bad writers he notices their lapses of taste at once. He sees that they dwell on things Shakespeare would not have dwelled on, at his best, not because Shakespeare failed to notice them but because he saw their triviality. (Except to examine new techniques, or because of personal friendship, no serious apprentice should ever study second-rate writers.)

To write with taste, in the highest sense, is to write with the assumption that one out of a hundred people who read one's work may be dying, or have some loved one dying; to write so that no one commits suicide, no one despairs; to write, as Shakespeare wrote, so that people understand, sympathize, see the universality of pain, and feel strengthened, if not directly encouraged to live on. This is not to say, of course, that the writer who has no personal experience of pain and terror should try to write about pain and terror, or that one should never write lightly, humorously; it is only to say that every writer should be aware that he might be read by the desperate, by people who might be persuaded toward life or death. It does not mean, either, that writers should write moralistically, like preachers. And above all it does not mean that writers should lie. It means only that they should think, always, of what harm they might inadvertently do and not do it. If there is good to be said, the writer should remember to say it. If there is bad to be said, he should say it in a way that reflects the truth that, though we see the evil, we choose to continue among the living. The true artist is never so lost in his imaginary world that he forgets the real world, where teen-agers have a chemical propensity toward anguish, people between their thirties and forties have a tendency to get divorced, and people in their seventies have a tendency toward loneliness, poverty, self-pity, and sometimes anger. The true artist chooses never to be a bad physician. He gets his sense of worth and honor from his conviction that art is powerful—even bad art.

For all these exercises, avoid the cheap, obvious, and corny. For example, in exercise 3, don't write a sentence built almost entirely of adjectives. In other words, don't waste time.

1. Write the paragraph that would appear in a piece of fiction just *before* the discovery of a body. You might perhaps describe the character's approach to the body he will find, or the location, or both. The purpose of the exercise is to develop the technique of at once attracting the reader toward the paragraph to follow, making him want to skip ahead, and holding him on this paragraph by virtue of its interest. Without the ability to write such foreplay paragraphs, one can never achieve real suspense.

2. Take a simple event: A man gets off a bus, trips, looks around in embarrassment, and sees a woman smiling. (Compare Raymond Queneau, *Exercices du Style*.) Describe this event, using the same characters and elements of setting, in *five* completely different ways (changes of style, tone, sentence struc-

ture, voice, psychic distance, etc.). Make sure the styles are *radically* different; otherwise, the exercise is wasted.

3. Write three effective long sentences: each at least one full typed page (or 250 words), each involving a different emotion (for example, anger, pensiveness, sorrow, joy). Purpose: control of tone in a complex sentence.

4a. Describe a landscape as seen by an old woman whose disgusting and detestable old husband has just died. Do not mention the husband or death.

4b. Describe a lake as seen by a young man who has just committed murder. Do not mention the murder.

4c. Describe a landscape as seen by a bird. Do not mention the bird.

4d. Describe a building as seen by a man whose son has just been killed in a war. Do not mention the son, war, death, or the old man doing the seeing; then describe the same building, in the same weather and at the same time of day, as seen by a happy lover. Do not mention love or the loved one.

5. Write the opening of a novel using the authorial-omniscient voice, making the authorial omniscience clear by going into the thoughts of one or more characters after establishing the voice. As subject, use either a trip or the arrival of a stranger (some disruption of order—the usual novel beginning).

6. Write a novel opening, on any subject, in which the point of view is third person objective. Write a short-story opening in this same point of view.

7. Write a monologue of at least three pages, in which the interruptions—pauses, gestures, description, etc.—all clearly and persuasively characterize, and the shifts from monologue to gesture and touches of setting (as when the character touches some object or glances out the window) all feel rhythmically right. Purpose: to learn ways of letting a character make a long speech that doesn't seem boring or artificial.

8. Write a dialogue in which each of the two characters has a secret. Do not reveal the secret but make the reader intuit it. For example, the dialogue might be between a husband, who has just lost his job and hasn't worked up the courage to tell his wife, and his wife, who has a lover in the bedroom. Purpose: to give two characters individual ways of speaking, and to make dialogue crackle with feelings not directly expressed. Remember that in dialogue, as a general rule, every pause must somehow be shown, either by narration (for example, "she paused") or by some gesture or other break that shows the pause. And remember that gesture is a part of all real dialogue. Sometimes, for instance, we look away instead of answering.

9. Write a two-page (or longer) character sketch using objects, landscape, weather, etc., to intensify the reader's sense of what the character is like. Use no similes ("She was like . . ."). Purpose: to create convincing character by using more than intellect, engaging both the conscious and unconscious mind.

10. Write a two-page (or longer) dramatic fragment (part of a story) using objects, landscape, weather, etc., to intensify two characters, as well as the relationship between them. Purpose: the same as in exercise 9 but now making the same scenic background, etc., serve more than one purpose. In a diner, for instance, one character may tend to look at certain objects inside the diner, the other may look at a different set of objects or may look out the window.

11. From exercise 10, develop the plot of a short story.

12. Describe and evoke a simple action (for example, sharpening a pencil, carving a tombstone, shooting a rat).

13. Write a brief sketch in the essayist-omniscient voice.

14. Write three acceptable examples of purple prose—that is, highly self-conscious and arty prose made acceptable by subject, parodic intent, voice, etc.

15. Write a brief passage on some stock subject (a journey, a landscape, a sexual encounter) in the rhythm of a long novel, then in the rhythm of a tight short story.

16. Write an honest and sensitive description (or sketch) of (a) one of your parents, (b) a mythological beast, and (c) a ghost.

17. Describe a character in a brief passage (one or two pages) using mostly long vowels and soft consonants (*o* as in "moan," *e* as in "see"; *l*, *m*, *n*, *sh*, etc.); then describe the same character, using mostly short vowels and hard consonants (*i* as in "sit"; *k*, *t*, *p*, *gg*, etc.).

18. Write a prose passage that makes effective and noticeable use of rhyme.

19. Write the first three pages of a tale.

20. Plot each of the following: a short-short story, a yarn, a fable, a sketch, a tale, a short story, an energeic novel, an architectonic novel, a novel in which episodes are not causally related (allegorical or lyrical structure, for example), a radio play, an opera, a film that could only be a film.

21. In a fully developed monologue (see exercise 7) present a philosophical position you tend to favor, but present it through a character and in a context that modifies or undermines it.

22. Write a passage using abrupt and radical—but thoroughly acceptable—shifts from the authorial-omniscient point of view to the third person subjective.

23a. In high parodic form (in the way Shakespeare seriously parodied the revenge tragedy in *Hamlet*, for example), plot one of the following: a gothic, a mystery, a sci-fi, a Western, a drugstore romance.

23b. Write the first three pages of the novel plotted in 23a, using the trash form as the basis of a serious piece of fiction.

24. Without an instant's lapse of taste, describe a person (a) going to the bathroom, (b) vomiting, (c) murdering a child.

25. Write a short piece of fiction in mixed prose and verse.

26. Write, without irony, a character's moving defense of himself (herself).

27. Using all you know, write a short story about an animal —for instance, a cow.

28. Write a short story about some well-known legendary figure.

29. Write a true story using anything you need.

30. Write a fabulous story using anything you need.

Index

A NOTE ON THE TYPE

This book was set on the Linotype in Janson, a recutting made directly from type cast from matrices long thought to have been produced by the Dutchman Anton Janson, who was a practicing type founder in Leipzig during the years 1668–1687. However, it has been conclusively demonstrated that these types are actually the work of Nicholas Kis (1650–1702), a Hungarian, who most probably learned his trade from the master Dutch type founder Dirk Voskens. The type is an excellent example of the influential and sturdy Dutch types that prevailed in England up to the time William Caslon developed his own incomparable designs from them.

Composed by The Maryland Linotype Composition Co.,
Baltimore, Maryland

Printed and bound by The Haddon Craftsmen, Inc.,
Scranton, Pennsylvania

Typography by Joe Marc Freedman